KORN

KORN

life in the pit

Leah Furman

St. Martin's Griffin ≈ New York

Design by Jane Adele Regina

www.stmartins.com

Library of Congress Cataloging-in-Publication Data

Furman, Leah.
    Korn : life in the pit / Leah Furman.
        p. cm.
    ISBN 0-312-25396-6
    1. Korn (Musical group) 2. Rock musicians—United States—Biography. I. Title.
ML421.K67 F87 2000
782.42166'092'2—dc21
    [B]   99-045233

First Edition: May 2000

10 9 8 7 6 5 4 3 2 1

CONTENTS

introduction: korn—again rock   1

1 here sprout the seeds of diskord   7

2 kollision kourse with korn   25

3 kiddie what?!   39

4 got our mojo working   45

5 the road warrior's booty   59

6 bumper krop   79

7 let 'em eat korn   85

8 the agony and the ekstasy   105

9 we're not going to settle   117

10 a korner on the market   139

11 krowned and dangerous   163

acknowledgments   183

about the author   185

INTRODUCTION
korn-again rock

In the none-too-distant past, America's leading music pundits were already sharpening their pencils, readying themselves for the inevitable call to arms that would have them eulogize a dearly departed genre—hard rock, or as *Rolling Stone* recently dubbed it, asshole rock.

The *Billboard* charts, covered as they were with a zodiac of names from the hip-hop, peppy pop, and alt-rock carpetbaggers' communities, offered little hope in the way of a hardcore revival. For if the greed decade had been all about excess, the 1990s were all about extremes. When the tide turned to Seattle, it left room for neither the infinite crop of hair bands nor the wave of heavy metal they rode in on. Washed up, reduced to a punch line, and relegated to the farthest reaches of the magazine stands and the no-man's land of MTV's *Headbanger's Ball*, heavy music was expected to play against type, and to slip quietly into that good obscurity.

Who can say what might have been had the Bakersfield Five not forced the backward-looking metal industry to reevaluate its modus operandi? With no regard for the law or their place in the established order, frontman Jonathan Davis, axmen James "Munky" Shaffer and Brian "Head" Welch, bass player Reggie "Fieldy" Arvizu, and drummer

David Silveria, collectively known as Korn, pulled off a veni, vidi, vici, making the return of thrash metal a fait accompli.

Even as Korn were just beginning to make themselves heard, howling "Are you ready?!" at a record-buying public numbed by happy ska and watered-down grunge, the overall landscape gave no sign that the answer would come in the affirmative. For all the quintet knew, an echo—reverberating within the vastness of the hardcore abyss—would be the only response they were ever going to get.

The band's aggressive stance belied their uncertainty and fear. "We wrote that shit and we were scared," recalled Fieldy. "We were like, 'We love this, but what are people gonna think?'" With a diabolical blend of schizoid seven-string guitars, maniacal forked-tongue vocals, bludgeoning bass, and pummeling drums, there was only one thing to think: "The horror! The sweet, fucking horror!"

Korn was about as far from pop as a disaffected teen could run. Album after platinum album, the quintet delivered a blitzkrieg on the eardrums. There was no muffling the racket, and parents would have been no less aghast had an obscene caller shown up at their doorstep and smiled. For all intents and purposes, Korn was that heavy breather, infiltrating America's homes with all the angst of their spine-tingling lyrics.

Striking fear into the heart of the Bible Belt is no mean feat. For their impudence, the men of Korn have had to pay in pain. Their Puma track suits, basketball jerseys, and generally slipshod sartorial style are more a hard-labor uniform than an effect to impress the ladies. Not that there were many ladies to impress in the early days.

From the beginning, the music of Korn has been an

homage to 'roid rage. Each concert would end in a heap of sweltering bodies, concertgoers spent from mirroring Korn's death-defying onstage antics. A blur of flying dreads, flailing arms, and banging heads, the quintet's high-octane performances made their albums look tame in comparison.

As if to prove that rabble-rousers' work is never done, the band carried on at this breakneck pace for over a year. From the blistering heat of the Southwest to the muggy humidity of the Northeast and back again, the Korn tour bus continued its cavalcade until no ear was left unbent. Whatever the damage incurred in maladies such as exhaustion and the like, the result was well worth the superhuman effort. Korn came off their yearlong trek the certified monarchs of the underground music scene.

With fans numbering in the millions, the band managed to retain their subterranean standing with support— or rather the marked lack thereof—from MTV and major market radio. Branded unpalatable to the naked ear and unfit for human consumption, the group had no choice but to go directly to the source. Opening up for any band that would have them, Korn worked tirelessly, watching their fan base increase exponentially as they went. Yet even when their eponymous debut album went gold, the only people who'd had a taste of *Korn* were the 500,000 or so X-Games enthusiasts who'd dug into their Adidas-emblazoned pockets and paid good money to hear it.

The pure grassroots approach proved so effective that Korn's second album, *Life Is Peachy*, debuted at Billboard's number 3. Instead of putting a cap on the band's tremendous outlays of energy, the triumph served only to reinvigorate their relentless pursuit of fan gratification.

Korn proceeded to anticipate the whims of the hungry throngs by setting up a Web site and instituting "Korn's After-School Special." Every Thursday night, come rain or high water, anyone who cared enough to witness the very latest in Korn goings-on had only to invest their allowance in the RealMedia software, and then click their mouse to www.korntv.com. There, they'd invariably find the five chipper heroes kicking back ice-coldies, entertaining guests ranging from porno to rock stars, and, in short, displaying none of that Sturm und Drang that made their albums and live shows so gut-wrenchingly aggro.

Nothing shocking about that, save perhaps the startling revelation that Korn are as normal a bunch of guys as you're likely to find spouting sex and death-obsessed lyrics. No limos, no bodyguards, no red-carpet treatment, it doesn't take a stretch of the imagination to picture these guys showing up at their local supermarket—and carrying their own groceries.

While Korn aren't the only act to pull out every stop come album-release date, the boys from Bakersfield have a way of making each savvy career move look like an unprecedented, once-in-a-lifetime occurrence. Witness Korn Kampaign '98.

Whereas most artists wouldn't shy away from calling a publicity campaign by its proper name, Korn are notorious for their aversion to all things mundane. Less duplicitous than imaginative, the band sparked interest in what would otherwise have been a ho-hum series of autograph signings and grip-and-grin photo ops by likening the extravaganza to a political campaign.

Lured by promises of celebrity guests and Q&A sessions with the Korn huskers themselves, thousands of fans showed up at each record-store appearance—much to the dismay of the group's seminal fan base. Waiting on line to mingle with their longtime heroes, Korn's stalwart followers took in the motley scene. The sight of cell phones and VJ-autographed MTV T-shirts must have set off a silent, but no less disturbing, intruder alert, as Korn's champions felt the first pangs of what could only be described as territoriality.

"I don't want anybody to like—like the trendy people, all the young kids, people that don't understand what Korn is all about—I don't really want them . . . it's gonna be misunderstood," one fan griped, giving voice to the prevailing fear. "I don't really want them to go mainstream and get all cool with it or whatever."

Too late.

Skateboard Nation's best-kept secret was, in a word, out. By the time the Kampaign trail came to a halt, the renegade group's third album, *Follow the Leader*, had debuted at number one on the *Billboard* 200.

With their lead single, the jacked-up, BeeGees-inspired "Got the Life," enjoying wide TV and radio airplay, hundreds of Korn chat rooms and Web sites—boasting such nifty monikers as Kandy Korn, Kreamed Korn, and Kornography—cropping up all over the Net, and their very own arena-bound tour package slated to revolutionize the meaning of the word *festival*, the band had achieved the pinnacle of popular success without ever sacrificing their distinctly non-commercial sound.

Now gearing up for the release of their fourth album, Korn remain a band like no other. Still spewing invective, bucking the system, and straddling the cusp between cult hit and mainstream phenom, Korn will keep right on picking at their scabs, exposing old wounds and crying out in furious pain for your vicarious pleasure until such time as their fountain of emotion and rage runs dry.

1

here sprout the seeds of diskord

They see me coming through the [grocery] line and think, 'What's this guy do for a living?' Since my checks are out of L.A., they run these triple checks on me. They wonder if I have been to jail," Videodrone frontman Ty Elam once observed, of the home town he shares with the members of Korn. "Bakersfield's a growing metropolis, but there's still that small-town sense at times."

Pillars of small-town U.S.A. have always been adamant about keeping out the bad element, but Bakersfield, or B-town, as the natives affectionately refer to it, is no sleepy hollow of a hamlet. With a population fast approaching the 300,000 mark, a roster of schools that numbers in the hundreds, enough local radio stations to keep you fiddling with the tuner for hours on end, and not one blue law in the bunch, the city has every right to the designation of *metropolis*. But the town's many movie theaters, live-music venues, and watering holes prove only that while you can take the city into the country, you can't take the country out of a city—not out of this one anyway.

For all its modern amenities Bakersfield is an agrarian mining community. Located at the nethermost point of California's bounteous San Joaquin Valley, the outskirts of town are ripe with vineyards, almond blossoms, cotton fields, citrus groves, and dairy cows put out to pasture. Nearly a third of the city's breadwinners make their living off the land. A two-hour drive is all that separates the town from Los Angeles, but coupled with the area's entrenched rusticity, that hundred or so miles is more than enough to infuse B-town inhabitants with a sense of secluded isolation.

Comforting at its best, smothering at worst, the town lays claim to two equal and opposite types of denizen. Suffice it to say that for every "born, raised, and proud of it" Bakersfielder, there's one who's equally enamored of the "dying to get out alive" school of thought. Guess which of the two philosophies counted the future men of Korn as adherents?

"You can't make anything of yourself in Bakersfield, it's the armpit of the world and I hate it," Jonathan once railed. Another time, he got personal, referring to Bakersfield's narrow-minded townsfolk as "a lot of hicks. Crazy, white-trash people." The rest of the band was of the same opinion. As David explained, "In Bakersfield, there was not much to do. We had only two choices, making music or [going] completely crazy."

Still, Jonathan's boyhood plight was considerably more dire than that of his fellow kernels. While Munky, Brain, Fieldy, and David had somehow managed to coalesce into a garage band, and were left with a few fond memories of partying in the city's notorious "dirt-fields," Jonathan stood alone—and, true to David's assessment, went a little crazy in so doing.

As many Korn fans already know, the band's testosterone-fueled anthems of ear-splitting wrath are inspired by the early life experiences of one Jonathan Davis. The product of a broken home, an asthmatic, a victim of child abuse, and a perennial outsider, Jonathan is the force of darkness that gave the nascent Korn their razor-sharp edge.

"The normal hell-childhood" is how Jonathan sums up his wonder years. Born of an actress/dancer mother and a musician father on January 18, 1971, he was stripped of the stability afforded most three-year-olds when his parents divorced. Jonathan's mother, it seems, had taken up with a local actor who was portraying Judas in a Bakersfield production of *Jesus Christ Superstar*. "He was such an asshole to me," Jonathan recalled, "but it still made me cry to watch him hang by his neck." To Jonathan's chagrin, the two married shortly after the Davis divorce had been finalized.

Rick Davis, Jonathan's keyboard-player father, was too busy chasing his dream of rock stardom to spend more than the rare three days with his son. "He did fuck me over," said an older and wiser Jonathan, in reference to his dad, "but I can understand why. When he left to go on the road, he needed to put food on the table. He needed to pay hospital bills: I was asthmatic, I was in the hospital every month from the age of three to the age of ten."

Still, as Jonathan went on to say, "When you're three years old you don't think about that shit." Shuttled from his stepfather's to his grandparents' to his godparents', he felt abandoned, unwanted and cast aside. Despite the parental neglect, or perhaps as its direct consequence, the apple wanted to be just like the tree. No sooner had his parents split than Jonathan took up the drums—a Christmas present from his grandmother.

Flattered by the emulation of his young son, Rick Davis encouraged these efforts, going so far as to let the little tyke play with the grown-ups. "I started playing music when I was three, and I never lost the love of music, ever," Jonathan recalled. "My dad got me into music. He was in a band—a bunch of cover bands—disco, Top 40 stuff. I wanted to play drums. By the time I was five, I [had] played a couple of gigs with him—like two or three songs of the set. They'd let me in the bar and I'd get to play."

While his father's support of such musical enterprises would soon wane, Jonathan's passion for the art would persevere, seeing him through the bitter years that were still to come. A belief in guardian angels—fostered by his own paranormal encounters with his deceased great-grandmother and great-uncle, and reinforced by the theories of his astrologer aunt—also sustained the future nihilist. He grew up seeing ghosts ("They were like translucent white flashes of energy"), nearly becoming one himself when he was felled by a critical asthma attack at five years of age. "I died when I was a little kid, because I had asthma really bad. My heart stopped, and I didn't see no damn light or hear any music," he groused, ". . . maybe it wasn't my time."

The threat of physical death, however, would come to seem less ominous after Jonathan was thrown to the lions of grammar school, where he would die a million social deaths before clawing and fighting his way to freedom. From the outset of his schooling, it was apparent that Jonathan was not destined to win any schoolyard popularity contests.

Whether his alienation was due to his precarious family situation or to the introverted bent of his own personality, Jonathan found a convenient scapegoat in the form of the admittedly creepy, but decidedly innocuous Fred Rogers, of *Mr. Rogers' Neighborhood* fame. "When I was a little kid, Mr. Rogers is all, 'You've got to be nice and be honest and be a good person.' Being that way as a kid, I got fucking picked on and I was a nerd. I never got anywhere. I always got shit on! So fuck you!"

The abuse heaped upon young Jonathan's fragile frame

by the local youth was, no doubt, the source of countless hours of loneliness and despair. This all-consuming melancholia was punctuated only by the snippets of time he could spend immersed in the workings of instruments at his father's music store. Walking the aisles and watching as the music teachers gave their lessons, Jonathan was in his element.

Spotting an instructor between classes, Jonathan would immediately shift into action mode. "Would you show me how to play?" he'd ask. Not ones to turn down a request from the proprietor's progeny, the teachers would often oblige. "I would learn the basics for each instrument and then would teach myself the rest." In this manner Jonathan had become proficient in a number of instruments, including the piano, upright bass, violin, and the clarinet, by the age of twelve. If life wasn't perfect, it was, at the very least, bearable.

Then, as if to show that life would get substantially worse before taking a turn for the better, Mr. Davis remarried. The new woman in Jonathan's life was, in his opinion, the alpha and omega of wicked stepmothers, the type of woman who would yell at the boy just for coming home from school. With her arrival, picking the lesser of two evils—school life or home life—became a toss-up. "I fucking hate that bitch," Jonathan has since said. "She's the most evil, fucked-up person I've met in my whole life. She hated my guts. She did everything she could to make my life hell. Like, when I was sick she'd feed me tea with Tabasco, which is really hot pepper oil. She'd make me drink it by saying, 'You have to burn that cold out, boy.' Fucked-up shit like that."

Lying in his bed late at night, Jonathan would fixate on gruesome scenarios—picturing what he'd do if only the tables were turned—which invariably ended in his odious stepmother's drawn-out and painful demise. "In some sick way I had a sexual fantasy about her, and I don't know what that stems from or why, but I always dreamt about fucking her and killing her."

Long before Jonathan's warped visions of sex and death made Korn a household name, he was already less than two degrees of separation away from his future consorts. Despite its soaring population figure, Bakersfield was a small world where paths never failed to cross. In his days as an itinerant music man, the elder Davis had counted Reggie "Fieldy" Arvizu's dad among his bandmates. The fathers' camaraderie was not, however, to be visited upon their sons until the cruel politics of high school had turned to just so much water under the proverbial bridge. Aside from Fieldy, Jonathan was also acquainted with Brian "Head" Welch. "I knew Brian from junior high," he explained, "but I hadn't met Munky yet."

Although Jonathan had yet to meet both James "Munky" Shaffer and David Silveria, the two were well aware of the former's existence. They had both, oddly enough, dated his sister. While Jonathan eked out an existence on the fringes of the Bakersfield social scene, the four boys who would one day welcome him into their exclusive fold were already on close terms and jamming en masse.

Steeped in the tradition of Nashville and dubbed "Nashville West" in the 1960s, Bakersfield has had a country flavor ever since it gave rise to two of country music's most beloved figures. Back in the day, and even through the 1980s, Buck Owens and Merle Haggard had recorded simple, honest music for the salt-of-the-earth folk who tilled the soil from dawn to dusk, and wanted little more than a ditty to which they could have themselves a hoedown and skip to the loo come sundown. It was not a style that appealed to most Bakersfield teens, Munky, Brian, Fieldy, and Dave included.

In their neck of the San Joaquin, the kids wanted to groove with the latest Monsters of Rock. Heavy metal, workingman's music—that there was the thing. Anything resembling AOR or bearing the progressives' seal of approval was suspect in the land of the Korn. As the line of demarcation separating the real men from the circle-jerk instigators, rock 'n' roll was not to be trifled with.

The burgeoning musicians who were to become Korn couldn't quite reconcile themselves to this black-and-white vision of music, but understood the life-and-death import of keeping up appearances. "I listened to AC/DC, Mötley Crüe, and shit like that," recounted Brian, "but I liked everything. I'd watch MTV and want to learn a Tom Petty solo or a Cars riff. All those videos my friends hated, I'd dig, 'cause I wanted to do the solos. I never bought the record because I'd get laughed at, but I'd learn the solos."

Brian had begun on his path to musical glory by following in Tommy Lee's footsteps. His infatuation with the drum kit, much like that of Jonathan, would not withstand the test of time—thanks mostly to Mr. Welch's words of wisdom. Seeing his ten-year-old son's growing love for the drums, the elder Welch shook his head in parental concern. "Well, you can play drums, but would you rather haul around a huge-ass drum set or a guitar and an amp?" he reasoned with the lad. "Why don't you try the guitar and see if you like it?"

As chance would have it, Brian was already gaining an appreciation for guitar. He'd been listening to Queen's "Another One Bites the Dust" and getting off on the powerful chord arrangements. His father didn't have to ask twice. Within a month, Brian was playing the guitar and loving every flat-picking minute of it.

In a few years' time, Brian would gladly part company with his inaugural guitar, making a black-marketer's profit on the gullibility of aspiring axman, and first-class pigeon, James "Munky" Shaffer. "Actually, he sold me my first guitar—and he ripped me off! It was a Peavey Mystic, which looked like a big tooth," recalled Munky. "He sold it to me for three hundred dollars."

Knowing nothing about guitars or the fair-market values thereof, Munky thought he'd scored a bargain. Truth was, his main interest in the instrument lay in its restorative properties. A few months prior, he'd been told of an after-hours party, and naturally made it his mission to attend. But, being only fourteen at the time, getting from point home to point kegger took some doing. Under the cover of night, Munky mounted his rickety old three-wheeler bicycle and prepared to ride like the wind. Alas, just as he was about to slip out undetected, he heard the *rat-tat-tat* of a bike chain slipping off its sprocket. Shit.

To silence the infernal racket, bound to alert his parents and foil his plans for the evening, Munky acted on instinct. Without stopping to think, he clamped his left hand down on the chain.

"Aaarrrggghhh!" Next thing he knew, he was howling in pain. In his race for fun and adventure, Munky had lost the use of a crucial appendage—his finger. Caught between the chain and the teeth of the sprocket, his left index finger was a severed, mangled mess.

After being driven to the emergency room and undergoing a series of shots, stitches, and bandages, Munky, along with his perplexed parents, conferred with the physician. The prognosis was promising: The boy would be okay with the aid of painkillers and a little musical therapy. According to the M.D. on duty, the sensation in the injured digit would return faster if Munky took up an instrument for physical therapy.

Taking the prescription to heart, Munky waited only for the bandages to come off before going in search of a good deal on a used piece of equipment. The pursuit led him straight to Brian's locker. There, the high-school freshmen talked shop, with Head extolling the virtues of his Peavey Mystic, trying to fleece the novice for all he was worth. Years later, Brian is still gloating over the victory. "I played it for a few years and then I made my money back, and then some, on Munky."

Just as Brian's double-cross didn't escalate into any crisis of conscience, it didn't cause any bad blood between him and Munky, either. On the contrary, the latter quickly took to the guitar, becoming one of Brian's closest friends and his most arch of rivals. Soon Munky had even hatched a scheme to recoup some of the funds he'd lost on that Peavey Mystic. "Brian pretty much inspired me to start playing. I used to go over to his house and eat his mom and dad's food so I could save my lunch money and then buy an amp."

With some help from his new pal and his generous parents, Munky was well on his way to mastering the guitar. In time, it was Brian who was coming over to Munky's and getting blown away by his progress. Rushing home to brush up on his licks, he'd wait for his opportunity to turn the tables and impress Munky. "It wasn't competition," explained Brian, "but he'd see me as I was getting good and that would pump him up; then I'd see him a month later and he'd pump me up. We motivated each other that way."

Brian had yet another friend to spur on his efforts. Reginald Arvizu, alias "Fieldy," was a regular fixture in Brian's garage. Having inherited his dad's proclivity for the stage, Fieldy had been Brian's partner in raucous music-making ever since they'd first met in junior high. By Bako standards, Fieldy was something of an oddity, with musical tastes that ran toward the exotic. Instead of growing out his mullet and headbanging to the sounds of speed metal, the round-faced youngster grew up vibing to the deep grooves of funk and hip-hop acts such as Afrika Bambaataa and Parliament/Funkadelic.

It was only a matter of time before Brian realized that he could bring his two friends together. United by their love of music and their distaste for the B-town music scene, the three players would soon form a band that would provide them with an emotional outlet and sustain them through the mind-numbing boredom that prevailed in Bakersfield, California.

While Jonathan's friends-to-be were laying the groundwork for his future, Jonathan was moonlighting as an amateur recording artist. After securing a job with the Buckaroos, hometown hero Buck Owens's back-up band, and closing down his music store, Mr. Davis was able to buy his country-crooning band leader's former recording studio. Once all the visiting musicians had gone home, the lights were shut off, and the studio locked up for the night, that's when Jonathan would make his move. With his portable keyboard player in hand, he'd sneak inside and take full home-court advantage. "I'd get the keys, and go in there in the middle of the night and record my own songs. I wouldn't sell them—I'd just give them out at school and stuff."

Whether there remains any trace of Jonathan's earliest recording sessions is uncertain, but there can be no doubt that these clandestine efforts were heavily influenced by Jonathan's synth-pop heroes, Duran Duran. "I loved Simon LeBon's melodies; I loved John Taylor's bass playing. They were a bad-ass band. They conquered the world. I love that *Rio* album—that was the best one. *Arcadia.* I was off my rocker listening to that shit."

His love for the band went well beyond mere admiration. Jonathan wanted to *be* Duran Duran, emulating their flamboyant style as faithfully as he followed their music. Raiding his sisters' stash of five-and-dime maquillage, he'd paint his nails in the splashy hues of Wet 'n' Wild and Mary Kay, and use their kohl pencils to line his eyes. While such antics may have been par for the course in NYC, they did not wash in Bakersfield. "When I was in high school, I wasn't a jock, I was into art, drama, and music and I wore eyeliner, so I wasn't accepted."

In fact, it was the lack of popular acceptance that pushed Jonathan farther and farther down the road less traveled. Having muddled through grammar school and junior high with just one friend, he'd accepted the loneliness as a way of life, seeking not to fit in but to make the most of his social exile. Still, in those days, it wasn't easy being Jonathan Davis. For wearing cosmetics, he caught flak from all camps—his parents, the administration, and the student body. "I was into Bauhaus, Ministry, Depeche Mode, the Thompson Twins. Dude, I was a New Romantic! I was a sissy la-la. They even took me to the gay [students'] counselor just because I wore makeup. All the cheerleaders would come and try and pick up on me just for laughs. That hurt."

The constant gibes from the jocks at school were no less painful. Walking the halls of Highland High School, Jonathan would often find himself having to blink back his tears when confronted by the football jersey–wearing steroid brigade.

"Fuckin' faggot!"

"Queer!"

"Pussy!"

Nothing, not even the plaintive wail of his bagpipes, could drown out the cruel sound of those homophobic slurs resounding in his head. And yet, the pipe band did endow the would-be artiste with some measure of distraction. "My grandmother's Scottish and I always wanted to learn how to play [the bagpipes]," he explained. "When I went to high school they had a band there, and I started taking lessons. They were always bitching at me to play my bagpipes so I just did it."

What started out as a perfunctory task, however, soon blossomed into a straight-up labor of love. Jonathan began by joining the Highland High School Pipe Band, and taking lessons from the band's Scottish conductor. "I took some lessons there, learned how to blow on the thing, and then I went to a real teacher, who went to Scotland and learned. He was an old Highland guy, and I started competing after that, up and down the States at established gigs."

One would think that Jonathan, with his bedroomful of prize ribbons and awards plaques, must have been a real source of pride for his parents. Such, sadly, was not the case. Despite his admitted nerdiness, Jonathan could never be mistaken for either a bookworm or computer-science geek. At home and at school, he was always the problem child and resident black sheep, or, as the clinical psychologists call it, the "identified" patient. Hanging out with the so-called freaks and misfits, Jonathan frequented gay clubs and rarely ran from a fracas. "I used to go to parties and get into trouble and fights," he recalled of his days in Bakersfield. "Everybody fights. That's what you do for fun, go beat the shit out of each other."

The young man had no shortage of reasons for engaging in all that was destructive and antisocial, and disappointing his parents in the process. All things considered, it's a wonder that Jonathan didn't end up doused by a bucket of pig's blood on prom night. As if the presence of his stepmom were not enough, Jonathan's dad suddenly found Jesus and got saved. Having been raised within a religiously lax, Presbyterian household, Jonathan had become accustomed to getting away with a certain amount of impiety, profanity, and blasphemy. When Mr. Davis became born again, the old rules no longer applied. "After that, my father became a crazy, non-denominational Pentecostal thing. You know, those crazy people who lay hands on people and they pass out and stuff? He became a Holy Roller," he recounted. "I thought it was ridiculous. When I was sixteen, the priests also made my dad burn all of my Mötley Crüe posters and tapes. That sucked! I had to start listening to my tapes when he wasn't around."

Jonathan's newfound hankering for metal was not the only thing frowned upon by his father—his penchant for music-making also became unacceptable. In this case, however, Mr. Davis was reacting as much to his own demons as to the ones expounded by the Church of Christ. Having tried and failed in his own pursuit of success, he blanched at thought of seeing his son repeat his mistakes. "He flat-out refused to let me get [into the music business]," Jonathan recalled. "He kept saying, 'No, no, no, don't do that.' I wanted to be in music so bad."

Sublimating his own needs to please his dad filled Jonathan with still more anger. A musician at heart, he had been making the two-hour pilgrimage to the L.A. club scene since he was fifteen. Ever since his first trip into the big city, when he'd gone to see Cradle of Thorns (recently renamed Videodrone and signed to Korn's record label), Jonathan had been hooked on the feeling that accompanied leaving Bakersfield in the dust. "Shit, every time I'd come over the Grapevine [a freeway pass to L.A.], I'd be shaking I was so happy."

Outside of music, life held little interest—so Jonathan decided to look into death. A high-school sophomore, obsessed with horror films, nurturing a newfound interest in Goth music and positively brimming with morbid curiosity, Jonathan was struck by a wild idea. By landing a school-sanctioned gig as an autopsy assistant, "I could cut up flesh and not have to go to jail." Hoo-wheee!

Investigating the possibility turned up a wealth of opportunity. The town's Regional Occupation Program had just the thing, a job order for an autopsy assistant from the Kern County Coroner's Office. After going in for an interview, and impressing the brass with his zeal for the craft, Jonathan got the position, rolled up his sleeves, and dug in. "At first I was queasy; I'll never forget the sound of the scalpel cutting a body open. But it was so cool trying to work out how these people died."

For Jonathan, working at the coroner's was, at the very least, cooler than trying to scare up a good time in Bakersfield. "The only things to do there are get fucked up on drugs, join gangs, get arrested, fuck and have a kid," he declared. "There's no music scene at all."

Of course, his socially adjusted, soon-to-be bandmates had a different perspective. David Silveria, for one, felt that "the music scene in Bakersfield goes in peaks and valleys, but when it's on a high, there's a lot more happening there than people would think." David's induction into the agonies and ecstasies of band life came when he was just fourteen.

The chance to join a real rock outfit presented itself through word of mouth, which had a way of spreading like wildfire through the brush of Bakersfield. Head, Fieldy, and Munky had finally decided to form a band, putting out feelers in their search for the missing link— a drummer. Despite the fact that he was still a freshman, and the three guys were all upperclassmen, David decided to vie for his shot at playing with the big boys.

What David lacked in years, he made up for in skills. He'd been banging away at his drums since he was nine years old, joining the school bands and jamming with any friend with an instrument. Without so much as one lesson, he'd developed into quite an expert drummer. "I started at around nine years old," David said. "I remember starting up the drums on my own and not being able to get my mind off them. I just listened to music and kept beats to it, and made up some of my own beats in my head. I didn't get my first kit until I was thirteen. I started playing in the school bands then, too, but I picked up the drum set on my own. Even then, I never really liked playing on my own—like sitting in the garage and practicing to records like other guys do. I was always more into playing with other people."

Social and outgoing by nature, David had no qualms whatsoever about calling the older guys to arrange an audition. All business, and professional beyond his years, he left a message expressing his interest in joining the ensemble on Fieldy's answering machine. "I get this message on my answering machine," Fieldy recounted on Korn's *Who Then Now?* video, "David's like fuckin' thirteen. It's like [raises his voice], 'Hey guys, looking for a drummer?' This little kid on my answering machine!"

While the guys may have entertained some doubts about the maturity and commitment of their would-be percussionist, when it came to drummers, Bakersfield's pickings were slim-to-nonexistent. Like Brian and Munky, most of the town's musicmen had eschewed the drum kit, modeling themselves, instead, after the gods of the screaming lead guitar.

They had to check out every lead. Piling into the car, the threesome and their gear hied on over to David's house, and set up their amps in his garage studio. After listening to the skinny wisp of a drummer wail away, it was obvious to all and sundry that David was as service-able a player as they were ever going to find. He was in.

Fieldy still remembers the first day young David arrived at his house for band practice—he was riding shot-gun in the family truckster. "When shall I pick you up, honey?" Playing with a kid barely out of junior high school seemed almost laughable at the time. Of course, there was nothing funny about the band's much-improved rhythm section, which proved once and for all that David's recruitment had in fact been a master stroke. "I kind of developed naturally as I went along, without worrying about it," he recalled. "I wasn't trying to copy anybody's songs or sounds. I just played my own way. I think I probably improved a lot mentally, just in the way I think about playing—coming up with ideas and then being able to play them on the drums."

The four-way collaboration would endure for the remainder of the crew's high-school years. The names of the bands and the musician rosters may have shifted here and there, but time after time, the quartet would find themselves reconvened. Together, they would make a rebellious brand of funk-metal that reflected their common need to bust out of Bakersfield. "We felt really limited," Munky explained. "We had this musical talent inside us that was hard to express in Bakersfield. It became this bottled-up anger. We decided to make music that captures that anger. Even after we moved away, we remembered how shitty it was to grow up there, and we draw on that for motivation."

Beckoned by the siren song of L.A.'s thriving club circuit, the guys felt like prisoners of small-town life. Paradoxically enough, they called their band LAPD. Coming of age in captivity had saddled them with enough pent-up tension to live up to their infamous name (which actually stood for Love and Peace, Dude), and each was counting the minutes until such a time as he could unleash his fury upon the unsuspecting ears of L.A.'s hardcore audiences.

2
kollision kourse with korn

In 1989, the Love and Peace Dudes finally made it over the freeway and into the promised land. Their Zion, as it turned out, was Orange County's punk-infested Huntington Beach. After plying the living daylights out of the Bakersfield live-venue beat, Munky, Fieldy, and David were ready to take a gun to their heads if it meant never seeing the inside of another local bar again. Just one hundred miles to the south, thrash culture had reached a fever pitch, and LAPD's heroes Faith No More and the Red Hot Chili Peppers were gaining vast, albeit underground, followings and blowing the roof off every joint they played. For a bunch of would-be up-and-comers who wanted little more than to rock until muscular atrophy set in, remaining in good ol' B-town would have been a safe but sorry way to carry on.

For a time, Brian "Head" Welch remained in Bakersfield, but the connection between him and his three erstwhile compadres remained intact. As soon as LAPD—fronted by one Richard Morral at the time—arrived in Huntington Beach, they found themselves up to their elbows in the blood-, sweat- and tear-draining process of "getting signed." According to David, "That's what it was all about back then. We had fans and people who came to the shows. We just had to believe that things were gonna get better and that somebody would notice us. We believed in ourselves, and it finally happened."

"It" was Triple X Records—an indie label that had released the first Jane's Addiction album back in 1987, and also played home to another Bakersfield-bred act, future Videodrones Cradle of Thorns. Enjoying the success they'd garnered via Jane's Addiction, Triple X was looking to add new names to their stable of artists. "At that point we were on top of the world, we had a hit record in Jane's Addiction, so it was pretty lucky for [LAPD] as well," recalls Triple X co-owner Dean Naleway. "These little kids, they were pretty much lucking into a recording contract. I could most definitely sense all the talent there. But they were at that point just a little baby band."

Naleway first came upon LAPD as they were rehearsing in a "little, tiny rehearsal studio." Word of the group had apparently spread to all the right people. Hunt Sales, sometime drummer for both David Bowie's Tin Machine and Iggy Pop, had heard of the LAPD through Arthur Von Blomberg, a mutual acquaintance. "I was working with Hunt on different projects," recounts Naleway, "and he told me that his friend Arthur had a band that I should probably check out. So I went down, and I heard their songs and I liked them . . . David was just so naturally talented, it was just amazing. I mean, him and Reggie, that rhythm section together was just incredible. I mean, from the first time I saw them I knew I wanted to work with them . . . So, we agreed to do a record together."

While the small label was unlikely to equip the ensemble with a promotional budget worthy of the *Billboard* Top 50, getting a record deal was, in itself, a source of tremendous affirmation and relief for the struggling outfit. With thousands of other musicians/delivery guys glutting the city's nightclubs and pizza parlors, the men of LAPD were beginning to find the big, "What label?" question all too demoralizing. "They were poor, man," Naleway confirms, "they had just enough money to get something to eat. They all had little side jobs that they could really care less about, that they were doing just to get enough money so they could pay their rent and eat."

After years of polishing their act, posting their own bills, paying to play, and generally hanging on by the very skin of their choppers, Love and Peace, Dude were finally making headway. "LAPD really was good for us," mused David, "because we learned a lot about the industry and how things work. We played all the L.A. clubs—even some pay-to-play venues—for about two years. Even when we didn't pay to play anymore, we were playing for nothing, which is still paying to play. We definitely did not get a record deal after a few songs, we paid our dues."

A convivial label party, a long-awaited signing of the contracts, a warm round of handshakes, and the friendly flash of a camera served to commemorate the band's induction into the Triple X family. Finally, the group was legit—and not a moment too soon.

Back in Bakersfield, Jonathan was going through some trials and travails of his own. His first year in the coroner's trenches witnessed Jonathan taking a perverse pleasure in his work. Most people would never get to see death up close and personal—this was the dark side, and he "really loved it." Having taken such a shine to his work-study program, he decided to carve out a career in the decidedly gruesome field of mortuary sciences.

Music, however, had never strayed far from his mind. While he would forever remain loyal to the glamour-boy posturings of Duran Duran, Jonathan had moved on, first to the industrial beats of Ministry and Skinny Puppy, then to the Goth sobriety of Christian Death, until finally winding up a metalhead with a part-time gig as a hip-hop-spinning deejay. This musical sideline brought Jonathan into contact with like-minded peers, allowing him to expand his heretofore limited circle of friends. His desire to yield to the showbiz bug was immense, but his parents would invariably roll their eyes to the skies—as if to ask, "Have you learned nothing from your father's example?"—each time that he brought it up.

By this time, Rick Davis had divorced Jonathan's arch-nemesis of a stepmother. He'd also gone through a bankruptcy which had left him in penury. Attributing all of his financial and emotional discomfiture to his chosen profession, Jonathan's father looked at his son and said, "Always have a day job to fall back on."

Having already disappointed his parents one too many times, through a series of fights and a less-than-stellar academic track record, Jonathan's family ties were in jeopardy. Cast out of his home in 1989, the prodigal son knew what he had to do in order to right the wrongs of the past. Sure enough, after he enrolled in the San Francisco School of Mortuary Science, graduated with a degree and scored a job at the Kern County Coroner's Office, all was forgiven. As he later explained, "I worked for the county. I got paid from the county. They thought it was dope. They were proud of me."

On the surface, it seemed as though the Davises had every reason to be satisfied with their son's progress. In the course of a year, he'd effected a complete transformation, going from a shiftless ne'er-do-well, to a man with a five-year plan. Splitting his time between an embalmer's apprenticeship at a local funeral home and a job as an autopsy assistant at the coroner's department, Jonathan was on the fast track to earning his adult's stripes. "I'd be working in a funeral home and the coroner's office, because I wanted to be a deputy coroner, like a coroner cop—they don't do any of the cutting," he elaborated. "They just go to the scene and investigate and write up reports, which is fine. You get to carry a gun and get a badge and a cool car, shit like that."

And it wasn't as if Jonathan was not enjoying his job. Indeed, few things gave him as much pleasure as the sight of an undefiled corpse. "I had a sick obsession with embalming and autopsies," he admitted, "but I didn't want to fuck the corpses or nothing. I just got off on cutting people open. I could do things that serial killers did and get paid for it. I could hack up bodies."

With on-site lodgings, the possibility of career advancement, and a sizable paycheck to boot, the job seemed almost too good to be true—and, of course, that's exactly what it was. What Jonathan may not have known at the time was that his nights of working the graveyard shift at the morgue came replete with ghosts that, once encountered, could never be forgotten. Not surprisingly, disemboweling the bodies of children and former acquaintances was not always the sick rush Jonathan made it out to be. In fact, many was the time that it was downright spooky.

One evening, Jonathan was peaceably going about his business in the mortuary when he was interrupted by a frantic, middle-aged woman. Talking on the exhale, and visibly distressed, she proceeded to tell Jonathan her tale of woe. From her agitated ramblings, he was able to extract the eye of the dilemma; she was convinced that her daughter's husband was going to kill her daughter.

At first, the young apprentice didn't understand why she'd come to him, or what he was expected to do, but his heart went out to the woman. Jonathan couldn't bring himself to turn her away. Doing his best to help out, he tried to allay her anxieties with kind words and sympathy. He even called her daughter to make sure everything was all right. Finally he managed to calm her down.

Thinking he'd served his purpose, Jonathan gave her a hug and wished her well. "The next morning, I came in and she was lying there on the slab," he recalled. "She'd gone straight home and killed herself. I was freaked out so bad."

While the memory of that woman's once-vital body lying prostrate and lifeless would haunt Jonathan for the rest of his days, it is hardly the worst of his morgue-induced nightmares. "I've had even worse, I've had a ten-month-old baby who was fucked by [her] dad. With its legs totally broken back, just totally killed by fucking [her]. I've seen many things like that, so I've learned you just have to appreciate life and I've learned how people really are, and how this world is."

Eventually, Jonathan would go on to commemorate the child's passing in song. But this was 1991—Jonathan had yet to stumble upon his songwriter's voice. He'd have to bear witness to countless more calamities before he could truly learn the morgue's lesson and seize the day.

Besides being an exciting year for hard rock, with Guns N' Roses, Metallica, and Nirvana all working to raise the bar for future generations, 1991 also bore witness to the recording of LAPD's first LP, *Who's Laughing Now?* In the year since they'd inked the deal with Triple X, the band had put out a three-song EP, the self-titled *Love and Peace, Dude*. Produced by Arthur Von Blomberg, *Love and Peace, Dude* was released on vinyl and cassette in 1990. It was to be LAPD's first introduction to the world at large.

The response to the record had been promising enough to warrant a second foray into the studio. This time, however, Munky, David, Fieldy, and Richard were expected to deliver a full-length album. Benefiting by Dean Naleway's production capabilities and years of grueling rehearsal, the recording novices were undaunted by the challenge.

Recorded at Pen Dragon Studios in Redondo Beach, California, *Who's Laughing Now?* is as much a testament to LAPD's awesome potential as it is an expression of Fieldy's early musical vision. The bassist had taken the point on the LAPD album just as he would with all of Korn's subsequent LPs. "They're all talented, but I think Reggie had more of a knack for the songwriting," Naleway says. "A lot of the ideas came from Reggie. Richard was a good contributor, he wrote the lyrics. But as far as the song structures and the bass lines, the real meat-and-potatoes of the songwriting was coming from Reggie for sure."

Despite Fieldy's fat bass lines, the eleven resultant cuts were not what anyone would characterize as Korny. "We were still trying to find our own band sound and develop our own individual sounds on our instruments," David explained. "If you listen to those records now, you wouldn't think we were even the same guys playing on them. It was kinda a heavy, up-tempo punk, not at all what we're doing now."

While Korn had yet to germinate, the basis for the band—their standard songwriting procedures, notoriously dark sense of humor, and copious alcohol consumption—was already in place. No longer a ragtag group of country bumpkins, LAPD had toughened up considerably in the two years they'd spent in Los Angeles. This newfound sophistication was made manifest by a pronounced change of attitude. Suddenly the guys began telling people that LAPD stood not for Love and Peace, Dude (a name not itself wholly devoid of irony), but for Laughing as People Die.

According to Naleway, they "figured Love and Peace, Dude was getting kind of corny, they wanted it to be called Laughing as People Die. And we kind of talked them out of that 'cause that was kind of a little bit too much." As much as the band may have wished to rename themselves and their album Laughing as People Die, the last thing they wanted to do was alienate their benefactors. Deferring to the wisdom of the label execs was not a hard compromise as, heretofore, the rapport shared by Triple X and LAPD was one of good feeling—both in and out of the studio.

Dean Naleway fondly recalls the many "Miller times" that he'd shared with the strapped-for-cash artists while recording their first LP. "They didn't have any money, so we were, like, splitting McDonald's hamburgers," he says. "We had to make sure that we had just enough money for the beer that we needed for that day and whatever was left over, we'd buy McDonald's hamburgers."

Although tensions would eventually arise, conflicts between the band and their label would never have the chance to erupt into any egregious disputes. The sole difference of opinion, and the one that would ultimately lead to a parting of the ways, revolved around the band's backstage antics. When *Who's Laughing Now?* hit the streets in 1991, the group was ready to support their album; the same could not be said of L.A.'s club owners. Although the album was performing well enough in Europe and causing a small stir in the U.S., the quartet soon found themselves personae non gratis at quite a number of Los Angeles venues.

"We started getting them some live engagements and they were out playing around town, which was kind of a nightmare," Naleway admits. "They were pissing a lot of people off, they were into a lot of different mischiefs like breaking shit backstage, peeing in the dip, throwing food, just real immature kind of mischievous mischief. That was one of the problems that we had. We could have probably set up a European tour for them, but we wanted them to get their shit together here before we put our reputation on the line by bringing a band that was going to cause havoc over to Europe."

And therein lay the problem. Despite their label's vehement protestations, the guys of LAPD continued to desecrate one greenroom after the next. Appalled and disgusted by the band's drunken shenanigans, many club owners were up in arms. Those who took a lighter view of the backstage hijinks, however, found that the band had real drawing power. It had been some time since LAPD had had to rally all their buddies to avoid the kick in the wallet that low attendance figures delivered, and the guys felt ready to take their show on the road. *Kerrang!* magazine had given *Who's Laughing Now?* an encouraging review, and there was a real demand to be met in Europe.

"Europe is going to be out of the question unless you guys grow up some," Dean Naleway said, bringing LAPD's relationship with Triple X to an impasse.

"Fuck *that*," thought the musicians. At the ages of twenty-one and twenty-two, the guys still had plenty of wild oats left to sow. They weren't the only band of musical outlaws to hit L.A. although it seemed as though they were the only ones to be penalized by their record company. Was there no justice? Their entreaties fell on deaf ears. Triple X stood their ground. According to Naleway, "We got to a point as a record company, we had a lot of business going on, a lot of different bands we were working with. We were kind of frustrated with them just because of the antics and stuff at that point. There were some tensions and we just came to the point where we just mutually decided, 'Okay, let's just go our own ways.'" Translation: Babysitting was not high on the label's "to do" list.

Adding to LAPD's laundry list of complaints was the

series of problems they'd been having with Richard Morral (credited as Richard Morales on *Who's Laughing Now?*, the kind that would ultimately lead to the vocalist's abrupt departure. "They were just having growing pains, and some things came between them," Naleway explains. "Richard actually ended up quitting, which was the worst mistake he ever made."

As we shall soon see, Richard's loss, along with the dissolution of their recording contract, would turn into LAPD's windfall. After the frontman walked off, Fieldy, Munky, and David were left to fend for themselves. To fatten up their sound, they invited Brian—who'd already come out of his Bakersfield seclusion to play guitar at LAPD's gigs and pilfer their supply of potent potables—to join the outfit fulltime, and began tossing around new ideas for names. After passing on Crunchy Taters and settling on Creep, the only thing keeping the four friends from recording a demo and shopping around for a new label was a lead vocalist.

There comes a time in every man's life when he wakes up only to discover that he is following the path of least resistance. For Jonathan, that point came when he realized that his work at the morgue was his parents' idea of a real job, not his. After spending two years trying to live up to his family's expectations and denying his own zeal for rock 'n' roll, he was finally ready to hang up his coroner's smock—at least long enough to join a local band.

Truth be told, whatever thrill he may have found in his work at the beginning, it had long since worn thin. The whiff of decaying flesh could start all manner of ghouls creeping out of the woodwork. "A motherfucker fucked dead bodies," Jonathan remembered. "This guy, he was a freak. Every time I'd go to the mortuary to drop off bodies, he was all [*creepy voiced*], 'Hi, Jonathan, how are you? How are you? come here . . .' And he'd always be rubbing me."

But laypeople did not have a monopoly on the freakishly profane. Men of the cloth, as Jonathan soon found, were some of the worst offenders. While his mother's remarriage had seen Jonathan baptized as a Catholic, the wisdom of his skepticism was confirmed when some priests mistook him for an innocent altar boy. As he subsequently explained, "I was working at the mortuary so I got to be around the clergy a lot. That's when I found out that religion in general is really just wack. I totally believe in God and Jesus and all that stuff, but I worship them in my own way. I don't believe in organized religion—I dealt with them hand in hand, and a whole bunch of Catholic priests tried to molest me. Telling me I was gay and I should go home with them and stuff."

Hazardous working conditions such as these movitated Jonathan to get off his ass and, pardon the pun, join the living. But, in the final analysis, it was the seemingly endless procession of tragic deaths that passed beneath his scalpel that deserves credit for driving the "carpe diem" point home. "I cut up people that I knew: drug overdoses, car accidents, a guy who died when a typewriter fell on his head. That kind of stuff shows you you could die at any minute."

Suddenly Jonathan was struck by the import of living every day as if it were his last. Of course, he'd long since understood the hackneyed concept. However, it's one thing to comprehend intellectually, and quite another to actually feel. Brooding more and more upon the subject of mortality, he decided that life was too fleeting to be squandered upon trivial pursuits. His search for meaning led him straight to an astrologer's doorstep. Since the psychic he sought out had taught his aunt all she knew about reading the stars, Jonathan had it on good authority that this woman was the real deal.

During his interview, the astrologer went into great detail predicting Jonathan's life story. According to her celestial prophecy, music would turn his life around. Here was all the incentive the heretofore would-be coroner needed to follow through on a lifelong dream. "I'm young and I'm going to do it now," he thought to himself. "If I don't, I'll end up being fifty years old, cutting people up, and kicking myself in the ass."

What, after all, was the worst that could happen? Jonathan figured that even if the astrological forecast proved fallacious, and he failed at rock 'n' roll, he could always return to the coroner's office. Death wasn't going anywhere; his youth, on the other hand, was slipping away with each passing day.

Once he'd made up his mind, the pieces to Korn's enduring legend were quick to fall into place. Within a few weeks, he was dividing his time between the morgue and a Bakersfield band called SexArt. Jonathan had hooked up with the band after meeting guitarist Ryan Shuck at, of all things, a local beauty college where Shuck was a student and haircuts were free. "He was my guinea pig," recalled Shuck. "He came in once from the coroner's office where he was working, and he had blood on his sleeve. He was trying to roll up his sleeve and hide it, the disgusting bastard."

After signing up to front Shuck's band, Jonathan found that he had a real knack for manning the mike. "I had no clue what I was doing—[the sound] just came out and people liked it. It just developed 'cause I didn't know what the hell to do with my voice." Although he has since described the ensemble as an "a Ministry–meets–Pearl Jam rip-off band," saying that "it really sucked," it was SexArt that opened Jonathan's eyes to the future: Music was going to be his main event, his parents' objections be damned.

Early in 1993, Brian and Munky paid a friendly visit to their Bakersfield-based relations. As it was not their band's search for a frontman so much as the complaints of their neglected families that had sent the two scurrying back to the scene of the crime, their inadvertent discovery of Jonathan Davis lends credence to the old adage "watched pots never boil." For some months now, Creep had been scouring the city in their quest for a lead singer. They'd tried out one contender after another, and still found no one who could live up to their lofty professional standards. Running dangerously low on funds, Brian was actually considering remaining in Bakersfield and taking his father up on that gas-station job he'd been promised, when he and Munky sauntered into a local dive for a spot of lager.

Having wet their whistles and shot the shit, the two were literally on the verge of crossing the threshold when something stopped them dead in their tracks. SexArt had taken the stage, and Jonathan had just begun to sing. The two looked at each other in disbelief. That voice . . . It was like nothing either had ever heard before, or since.

"Oh my god," Munky said.

"I know," Brian said.

Turning around, the musicians–cum–talent scouts walked back to their seats, never once taking their eyes off of Jonathan. His vocals, his energy, his whole onstage persona held Brian and Munky in a viselike grip for the duration of the set. They were transfixed. With the show over, the spell was lifted, and the guys were free to walk over to where Jonathan was standing. Complimenting him on the performance and restricting their conversation to SexArt, the two were sending out feelers to find out whether Creep had any chance of stealing Jonathan away from his Bakersfield outfit. "I didn't even have a clue that they were checking me out," recounted Jonathan. "They just said they liked my band a lot, and then I got a phone call the next day from another band giving me their phone number to call them. So I did it."

While Jonathan deliberated, wondering whether he had it in him to leave his SexArt mates in the lurch, Head and Munky hightailed it back to Los Angeles to fill in the rest of the crew on the latest developments. Listening to their friends rave about the singular quality of Jonathan's vocal delivery, Fieldy and David were sold. The ball was Jonathan's to drop.

3
kiddie what?!

Inside of a month, Jonathan was driving down the Grapevine on his way to sunny Huntington Beach, California.
He found Munky, David, Brian, and Fieldy assembled and
anxiously awaiting his arrival in a categorically ungla-
morous apartment. Ever since their record contract had
expired a little more than a year before, the guys had been
scrounging to make ends meet. But much as Creep needed
a singer, they still had their reservations about Jonathan.
"When he came to the band, he was . . . he was . . . Ohhh,
man. In his old band, he used to wear skirts," exclaimed
Fieldy. "Dresses and shit," added Munky. "And makeup
and stuff—he used to dress like a girl," Fieldy continued.

Neither was Jonathan convinced. With a cushy job, a
band that shared his sartorial flair, and his parents' approval all waiting for him back in Bakersfield, the vocalist
had a good mind to stay put. Had it not been for that
eerily prophetic astrological reading he'd received three
months ago, Jonathan's loyalty to SexArt might very well
have kept him from auditioning altogether. "I didn't want
to betray my band," he said, "but I really listened to what
the astrologer said, and it made sense."

One look around Creep's roughshod digs, and a few

minutes of chitchat, told Jonathan that if he decided to stay on, he'd have his work cut out for him. "I knew I had to pay my dues when I started all of this. Fieldy was cleaning carpets. David had a gig at Pizza Hut. Brian and Munky worked at a furniture-moving company."

Had the audition not gone down like a house on fire, Jonathan would certainly have made a beeline back for B-town. Luckily the good vibrations began to flow as soon as Jonathan walked through the door. Talking to the guys of Creep, he sensed that they were serious about their work, and about each other. "When we first got together, we felt the commitment," Jonathan said. "We knew this was right. We knew we were a team and the vibe was there."

After the preliminary bonding had been taken care of, it was time to turn on the stereo, plug in the dinky Radio Shack microphone, and give Jonathan's pipes a good, long listen. He'd already had a chance to hear Creep's tape and think about his audition. This time, his vocal style would be different than that which Munky and Brian had had a chance to observe in their hometown bar. "I was into Duran Duran, Missing Persons, A Flock of Seagulls, that kind of vibe," Jonathan explained. "So when I joined this band, I had no clue what to do. I hadn't ever listened to heavy music. I just opened my mouth and hoped for the best."

Listening to Jonathan's possessed caterwauling, the quartet knew (the way a seasoned musician knows about a good piece of equipment) that this was their man or, as Munky would later call him, "the blessing of God." "He came down and started singing and we all just knew, right there," David attested.

Fieldy couldn't have agreed more. "When he came to try out for us, and we played a song for him, he just sang it from beginning to end . . . freestyle," he recalled, "and we knew. Even before he was done we were like, 'You're in. You're in the band.' Just like that."

After jamming with the homeboys, Jonathan, too, was a believer, and SexArt, along with Creep, were just two footnotes in the annals of rock music.

Much to the chagrin of his well-meaning parents, Jonathan swapped his steady gig at the coroner's office for a steady diet of Top Ramen and squatters' rights at someone's Long Beach garage. When Rick Davis drove down from Bako to hand over the belongings his son had left behind, the sight of Jonathan's makeshift dwelling brought tears to the grown man's eyes. As squalid as the situation seemed, the elder Davis couldn't help suffering some pangs of envy, thinking, "At least he's pursuing his dream."

While Jonathan had been quick to sever his ties with Bakersfield, a few relics did remain, namely, his girlfriend Renée Perez, his pain, and a nasty penchant for methamphetamines. At home, seeing as there wasn't much in the way of intellectual stimulation, speed had been easy enough to procure, but it wasn't until he repaired to Long Beach and befriended a speed dealer that Jonathan's hankering took on the character of a true addiction. "It's just being up," he explained. "If I didn't have to sleep, I'd love it. If I could just stay awake and there was no such thing as sleeping . . . there's not enough time."

To be sure, with Jonathan in the equation, the band had indeed become an all-consuming job. In comparison to their present exuberance, Creep looked like a half-assed, last-ditch effort. Within two weeks of Jonathan's arrival, the guys had been so inspired as to record demo versions of four new songs, "Blind" and "Daddy" among

them. A feeling of invincibility permeated the rehearsal
studio, as all five musicians came to the simultaneous realization that they had finally found their voice.

Right from the beginning, it was obvious that the quintet thought as one five-headed organism. "They had a hap-
pier groove before I joined," Jonathan recalled. "I brought
out the darker elements in them. It clicked." Free of fool-
ish pride, the rest of the group is of the same mind on the
subject, unfailing in giving their frontman his due. "We
feed off of Jonathan's energy," Munky confirmed. "Then
we give him the heavy music right back."

The addition of Jonathan brought new life into the
group, giving David his first taste of ambition and a sense
of purpose. Until now, the drummer had never known
the many joys of entertaining platinum-record wishes and
arena-headlining dreams. "I always liked playing, I mean,
there was nothing else I really wanted to do. But I don't
think I really took it seriously until Korn."

Korn, as the whole of slam-dancing America well
knows, is the name that symbolized Creep's graduation to
the inner sanctum of music-industry power hitters. Oddly
enough, it is also the moniker that attests to the band's
Farrelly Brothers–loving, Joe Adolescent identity. While
many would later speculate that Korn was short for "kiddie porn," the actual stomach-turning genesis of the name
is perhaps best left to its auteur. (Reader, be warned.)
"We had a party in Bakersfield," Jonathan recounted,
"and there were these two homosexual guys talking—
they were talking about how they were having sex with
each other. One guy was eating the other's butthole and
he blew diarrhea all over the other guy's face, and when
he opened his mouth he had a corn kernel on his tongue.
So, I used to walk around to people who knew the story
and say 'corn' to gross them out. It just stuck in my head.
I spelled it like a kid would."

Apropos of nothing, the handle and its empty-headed catchiness could not be denied. As soon as Jonathan made the suggestion, breaking in with a simple, "What about 'Korn'?" during a Budweiser-drenched brainstorming session, his bandmates were right there with him, rejoining with a resounding, "Fuck yeah!" Is there any doubt whether anything other than destiny could have brought this band of merry pranksters–slash–tortured artists together? Speaking for the whole crew, David explained the significance of "Korn" in *Who Then Now?* "It kind of means that it doesn't matter what your band's called. Name or not, the music makes a name, you know . . .'cause 'Korn,' that's a dumb name, but once a band gets established, then it makes a name cool."

This time out, there'd be no turning back. While Crunchy Taters may have morphed into Creep, and Love and Peace, Dude, into Laughing as People Die, Korn would be much more than another musical segue—it would be their ultimate climax.

By June of 1993, Korn had a four-track demo tape entitled *Niedermeyer's Mind,* and a producer in the person of Ross Robinson, their devoted friend and rabid supporter. Moreover, the guys had established both a killer songwriting MO and the type of easy camaraderie utterly devoid of the ego-tripping bullshit that had been, and would be, the Achilles' heel of many a great rock outfit. The chemistry was so powerful, the group dynamic so amicable, that it was as if Jonathan had been hanging with Fieldy, Munky, Head, and David all these many years—his memories of solitary despair but a wild figment of a frightened child's imagination.

Watching the quintet cavort into the wee hours, one would have to consult Jonathan's lyrics to unearth any trace of alienation and torment. Seeing as the singer's compositions were experiments in the channeling of "pure cathartic rage," it's easy to see why his downtime with the band smacked of high spirits and good cheer.

Judging by the short work Jonathan made of "Daddy," his most personally disturbing track to date, venting his spleen through song went hand in hand with joining Korn. The lyrics revealed a hitherto hidden chapter of the lead singer's childhood saga—his experience with sexual abuse. Contrary to what the title would lead audiences to believe, a neighbor had perpetrated the said crime, not Rick Davis. As much as he hated to discuss the intensely personal song, the shadow that it would eventually cast over his father's character would force his hand. "People think 'Daddy' was written because my dad fucked me up the ass, but that's not what the song's about," Jonathan elaborated. "It wasn't about my dad or my mum. When I was a kid I was being abused by someone else and I went to my parents and told them about it. They thought I was lying and joking around, so they never did shit about it. They didn't believe it was happening to their son."

The proof, as it were, is in the wailing vocals. Guided by the gentle prodding of demo producer Ross Robinson, Jonathan dug deep into the darkest recesses of his heart and came up with the kind of devastating delivery he's refused to replicate in live performance ever since. According to David, it was their wide-eyed, fresh-faced producer who made the difference. "Ross is a very pure and clean-spirited person," he said, "and you feel it when you're with him. He's the kind of person that can draw that out of you."

Although he'd never before occupied the producer's chair, Ross had been tight with the band since they'd transitioned from LAPD into Creep. He knew their sound, understood their vision, and badly wanted to break into record-producing. While Jonathan may have needed the extra nudge that only Ross could provide, the frontman is the first to say that his fellow bandmates, especially Fieldy, had not shared his desire for direction. With nothing to lose but their youthful exuberance, the songwriters took great risks, merged a dog's breakfast of styles, and came up with a tone so singular that it could only be described as unmistakably Korn.

———

"The sound just came out," recalled Brian. "We never tried to do anything special. Fieldy's into a lot of hip-hop, and me and Munky are hip to a lot of guitar shit like Mr. Bungle and old Cypress Hill." Jonathan would later agree with this "diverse influences" theory, saying, "We are what is going on now. I don't mean that in an arrogant way. What we talk about is here and now. This music is all of our influences plus our experiences. We aren't a band that tried to mix hip-hop, industrial, and metal, we're a blend of these sounds."

Knitting this strange brew of sounds into one cohesive aural sensation was a process as methodical and exact as the songs themselves were erratic and unpredictable. Although the media's gimlet-eyed focus on Jonathan would indicate that Korn is but a field trip into his bruised psyche, the whole is far greater than one of its parts.

Certainly, in the beginning, it had been Jonathan's fresh and uncommonly bleak perspective that had brought the band around to its new way of thinking. "When they heard my lyrics, it brought out more darker tones, started blossoming from there, we went with it, and the songs just decided to start growing," he explained, adding that "we're like a team because everyone in the band just takes it apart and makes it into a Korn song."

After quickly incorporating the new vocalist's Grim Reaperly persona into their calculations, the musicians took the lead, creating emotionally harrowing scores to bolster Jonathan's severe point of view. "Most of the time when we write, David, Munky, Head, and I will do all the music," recounted Fieldy, "and then Jon will come in and he won't write lyrics immediately—he'll sing a melody of just nonsense words and write lyrics later."

Jonathan described the standard operating procedure as follows: "When we write, someone plays something and everyone tries it and then we see if everyone's vibin' off it. If it sounds good, we'll keep goin' to another part. Sometimes we'll play it for four bars and then everyone's just doin' their own thing with it. We just all play it and it sounds like a big mess. Sooner or later, someone usually comes up with something cool. Then we just build the song from there. Sometimes we'll throw it away.... Sometimes we get parts together and we'll say, 'That's not that good.' Then two weeks or a month later, we'll try it again, or fit it into something totally different, and it'll work very well."

Clearly, Korn's approach to songwriting was no striking departure from the generally accepted format. The results, however, were by far the heaviest anyone had ever heard. Thanks to Munky's and Brian's seven-string Ibanez guitars, when these guys said, "Let's tune it down," they really meant it. "Fieldy got a five-string Ibanez bass when the band was getting started," recalled Brian, "and he told Munky he should check out one of their seven-string guitars because it had a low B. When I joined, I bought my first seven-string, too, and we developed from there. The seven-string brings out heavy riffing. It's the Korn sound."

But while sporting "the Korn sound" may impart instant status now, this was still 1993. Heavy was as out as a red-light district in Giuliani's Manhattan. After completing their four-song demo, the quintet threw themselves headlong into a California club tour, while Ross Robinson and their manager set about hawking the tape all over town. According to Jonathan, "People were too scared to touch it."

With no way of knowing how long that fear would last, Korn continued to terrorize small audiences up and down the coast, leaving strewn beer bottles, regurgitated food, urine-soaked onion dip, and ringing ears in their wake. A few months hence, major- and minor-label interest began to build. Apparently, Korn's particular brand of insanity was an acquired taste, requiring repeated exposures. Either that, or the decision-makers simply had to see the band live to believe it. "Then finally record companies started talking to us, wanting to sign us," recalled Jonathan, "and we got offers from Atlantic and RCA."

Now it was Korn's turn to be afraid. They'd heard all the horror stories, they knew about all the unhappy endings—bands dropped by their labels, bands bullied by their labels, bands not promoted by their labels . . . The list of gripes just kept on going. Unwilling to jump at the first, or second offer, Korn held out for that most elusive of beasts—a record company that would support them unconditionally.

Enter Paul Pontius.

The A&R rep for Immortal Records (a small and relatively young subdivision of the Epic Records behemoth) had begun staking out Korn's shows ever since he had heard their demo. After keeping silent vigil at no less than eight live performances, Pontius emerged from the shadows of the dimly-lit club scene and made himself known. Right from the get-go, the band knew they'd found themselves a family. "Before Immortal, we had a lot of different offers from different [labels], but Immortal just made us feel like home," explained Jonathan. "[Paul Pontius] was really cool, and he was saying that they would put one hundred percent behind this band. That was what got us really interested in the company, because we knew that it would take a lot of work and dedication from the label's end to break the band, and they were able to guarantee us that kind of backing."

The search was over. The hard labor, however, had only just begun.

Pre-production on Korn's eponymous debut commenced almost before the ink on their record contracts had a chance to dry. Booking long stretches of time in an Anaheim rehearsal studio, the musicians worked day and night, coming up for air only after they'd wrought the lethal riff and chord combinations that would make up such Korn classics as "Ball Tongue," "Clown," "Faget," "Shoots and Ladders," and "Helmet in the Bush." The tracks came out so well, they surprised even the songwriters. "We wrote a whole new amazing set of songs. They just came from our heart. They pretty much poured out—unwillingly—and it's amazing how it turned out," enthused Munky. "We didn't expect anything this great. I mean, we've been playing music for a long time and it's pretty incredible."

While putting the finishing touches on "Shoots and Ladders," the guys realized that something was missing. On a whim, they asked Jonathan to bust out the old bagpipes. At first, the idea of mixing elements of folk music into their cauldron of hardcore rock sounded funny, even ridiculous. Jonathan, for one, had long since given up any hope he might have had of parlaying his bagpipe-playing trophies into profits. But much to the band's general surprise, what had begun as a joke turned out to be nothing less than a stroke of genius. From that point on, the frontman would have two credits after his name: Jonathan Davis—Vocals & Bagpipes. It was just crazy enough to work.

Once the instrumentals were in place, Jonathan would take the finished arrangements and sequester himself behind closed doors. "I wait till the last minute," he confessed. "Once a song's done and all arranged, that's when I start writing lyrics for it. I just have to be alone."

With only his bottle of Jäger and his stash of crystal meth to keep him company, he would invoke the spirits of Childhood Trauma and rage against the inhumanity that had chipped away at his youthful innocence. Every last word, outpouring of emotion, and cry of despair sprung from his own bitter experience. Far from an anthem to hate crime, "Faget" is a call for tolerance, addressing the various issues that Jonathan dealt with as a result of his low standing on the high-school totem pole. "It's really about me going through high school being called 'pussy', 'queer,' and all that stuff, about getting picked on by all these jocks."

The concept behind "Shoots and Ladders" sprung from Jonathan's disgust with a society so corrupt at its core that it cannot sustain a truly pure soul for any extended length of time. " 'Shoots and Ladders' uncovers the hidden messages in nursery rhymes, the first songs many of us ever hear," he began. " 'Shoots and Ladders,' to set the record straight, calls out nursery rhymes for what they really are. I chose each rhyme for a different reason—'Baa Baa Black Sheep' has racist overtones. 'London Bridge' talks of all the people of London dying [from the Black Plague], as does 'Ring Around the Roses.' Then there's 'Little Red Riding Hood'—one story tells of the wolf raping Red Riding Hood and killing her." Of this track, Jonathan went on to note that "there is a lesson anyone for censorship should realize. The fact is you are covered from the world and once you are born into the world, your eyes open and it's all over."

While most of Jonathan's lyrics relied on experiences long since past, there were those songs, "Clown" for one, that dealt with the significance of more recent events. "We were playing a show in San Diego and this Skinhead guy came up and said, 'Fuck you! Go back to Bakersfield!' I didn't understand that and I bent down and he tried to swing at me. Our road manager Jeff knocked his ass out. So that song is 'Clown.' "

Often Jonathan would work straight through the night, snorting speed as if it were his asthma inhaler, and only taking breaks to blow off steam with his friends. While this self-destructive streak had actually begun in Bakersfield, long before work on *Korn* got under way, recording the album did much to exacerbate his drug problem. A few years hence, he'd admit as much: "On *Korn,* I wrote most of the shit on drugs, fucking methamphetamines."

The words to "Helmet in the Bush" reflect the fear that gripped the vocalist at the height of his drug problem. He begs for divine intervention to deliver him from his waking nightmare, as if he cannot even begin to help himself—and indeed, at the time he could not. "I'd wake up in the morning and do a line to get out of bed," he confessed. "Speed in the morning, I'd have it all lined up for breakfast so when I'd lay down and go to sleep, I'd wake up and just snort and it's like, 'Yeah, okay, I'm up.' It was bad. It's like, you do one line and stay up all night, but then you have shit to do the next day so you have to do another line to be able to keep staying up to get that shit done. Eventually you start spinning-out from sleep deprivation. You get hallucinations and shit like that."

At length, it was a strung-out and emotionally drained Jonathan that returned to his band. With lyrics in hand and producer Ross Robinson in tow, Korn was ready to go into phase one of production.

Situated along the picturesque Pacific Coast Highway, some thirty minutes north of the Los Angeles smog and traffic congestion, the beachfront properties of Malibu play host to the stars, the moguls, and the heirs to some of America's tidiest sums. The serene beauty of Steven Spielberg's and Robert Redford's stomping grounds is a far cry from the urban decay of Sunset Strip. Even Korn's arrival at Indigo Ranch Studios in the summer of 1994 could not disturb the quiet of this Western front. A fact that the band liked not at all—"It was green; you could pick fruits off the trees," Jonathan said, shaking his head. "You have to feel right to sing the songs. Malibu wasn't right."

Although the none-too-discreet charm of the setting was lost on the group, they somehow managed to adapt themselves to all that blasted verdure. Not only would most of *Korn* be cut at Indigo Ranch, but the band would live to record yet a second album at the Malibu studio. Certainly, the windowless confines of the recording studio must have played a part in the group's change of heart. Shut in from the outside world with the sounds of Pharcyde blasting from every speaker, they found the requisite motivation to assume their no-holds-barred persona.

Despite this flagrant antipathy toward shiny, happy Malibu, these guys had never stopped giving top billing to the pursuit of fun. As Jonathan has said, "This band's all based on fun. That's why we do it." Thus, raucous fits of laughter were as much a studio staple as Fieldy's percussive bass lines, David's tight rhythms, and the ax-wielding fiends' jarring twin guitars. With each member working and playing just as hard as ever, the serious subject matter seemed to have had no effect on the group's notoriously goofy dynamic. "Just because of our music and lyrics, people used to think everyone in the band was depressed or down as people," David would later relate. "People get the idea that we're on the verge of suicide at twenty-five. So when they meet us, it's like, 'Wow, you seem happy.' "

Making music they loved, signed to a label they trusted, and working with their best friends, the guys must have sensed that misery was well outside their rights. They had been working on this material for some sixteen months, with no guarantees. For all they knew, they could have been moving furniture and delivering take-out well into their late twenties. Suddenly their dreams were coming true. There isn't a psychologically sound band on the planet that wouldn't be having a field day. And, make no mistake, the men of Korn were sane—emotionally disturbed maybe, but definitely sane.

The Indigo Ranch sessions turned out to be yet another source of satisfaction. Fieldy, Munky, Brian, and David had their parts nailed, and the recording went down like clockwork. "I'd played the songs so much," explained David, "that my parts were already second nature by the time we went into the studio."

No sooner had the drum, bass, and guitar tracks been cut, than the group entered phase two of the recording process. They repaired to the only place in the world that could give a man like Jonathan Davis enough heebies to lay down his vocals.

Bakersfield.

Of course, once within the Bako city limits, only one studio would do—Fat Tracks. The site of Buck Owens's former triumphs and Jonathan's own clandestine recording sessions, Rick Davis's studio provided the ideal ambiance. Although the sound equipment was no testament to technological innovation, Jonathan's sole priority was the aura. He needed to get into the proper mind-set, and driving past the sites of his boyhood crises never failed to deliver a rush of painful recollections.

"Bakersfield is a very strange place," he explained. "I got this weird, sick, cool vibe doing vocals where [Buck Owens] did all his albums. I went to the heart of Oildale, which is white-trash central. You know, tweaked-out speedsters, the bars with chicken wire in front of the stage. That's the kind of vibe I needed."

For the purposes of this album, Korn couldn't ask for anything better than Fat Tracks. If Jonathan was going to shed his natural inhibitions and characteristic affability, and stay true to his lyrics, it would have to be within these walls. Digging around in the primordial ooze of one's subconscious is hard enough on its own, let alone for the benefit of innumerable record buyers. The frontman would need some help achieving the desired effect.

The responsibility for bringing Jonathan in touch with his early feelings of fear, anger, and pain fell to Ross Robinson. The producer was quick to resume the quasi-psychoanalytic tactics that he'd implemented on Korn's demo. "I've always been into working with the kid who was beaten up and kicked around," he said, "because the most creative stuff will come out of them. And that's Korn."

As Jonathan will attest, getting him to open up on that first LP was no easy business. But, by all accounts, the novice producer proved more than up to the task. "I fucking had a lot of shit on my mind a long time that I wanted to get out, and our producer, Ross Robinson, brought it out from me," recalled Jonathan. "I felt very safe with Ross."

Despite the constant flow of reassurance from both his producer and his bandmates, recording *Korn* was an ordeal that Jonathan would not soon forget. He'd go on to say that "recording the CD was horrible for me," and that it was "a very hard record to do." But then again, a masochist like Jonathan wouldn't have had it any other way. "I like being miserable," he admitted, only half joking. "I guess I'm punishing myself. I guess I punish myself every day. I don't know . . . I haven't really analyzed myself lately. I just like the pain."

Sure enough, the labor pains that accompanied the birth of the album were like so many battle scars, or stretch marks as the case may be—something the vocalist could always point to, as if to say, "See what I had to go through for you?" Not only had Korn completed their first

CD, but, in the final analysis, Jonathan was a better man for the experience. "It was a hard time for me, but liberating," he explained. "I feel better now, definitely."

All told, Korn had taken less than four months to record and mix their album. When they deposited the fruit of their labor on Immortal's doorstep, the label showed no signs of reneging on their promise to back the group. An October release date was set, and "Blind" was chosen as the single to lead up the festivities.

With a couple of months of thumb-twiddling inertia stretched out before them, Team Korn agreed to forgo the doldrums and make themselves useful. The group was rarin' to delve headlong into their promotional trek, and start building interest among the great unwashed. Their management stayed on top of the situation by getting Korn supporting act gigs with House of Pain as well as Biohazard. "We were stoked that we got a tour," Jonathan said, "and we didn't really care who we went out with as long as we were out getting a chance to play. That was all that mattered."

Before they set off for the open road, however, Korn had to tie up a few loose ends. Not the least of these was their band logo, which should have been positioned to best advantage on their drum kit and their forthcoming album, but was instead conspicuously absent. The trademark's childlike scrawl and dyslexic *R* was Jonathan's brainchild. When their manager informed them that they'd need a logo, "I did it in about two seconds," he recalled, "the whole gross story about our name had a very kid vibe about it. The whole basis for that album was growing up and being a kid, so I took a big black crayon and did that in two seconds left-handed."

After collaborating on the menacing theme of their CD's cover art and sitting for a group mug shot, the guys left their label with specific instructions to keep the lyrics out of the liner notes. Like a true abstract artist, Jonathan felt that to include the lyrics would be to do the listeners a grave disservice—he wanted his words to guide, not dictate, the record buyers' perceptions. "It seems like when I get a CD, I'm listening to lyrics and I'm reading," he opined, "I'm just reading 'em, it's like, 'Okay, that's it.' I think music's something that every individual has their own meaning to the song. They can come up with whatever the hell I'm saying and that's the beauty of it and that's what I wanna keep there."

That done, the group was free to go on tour with the rap ensemble House of Pain. The year and a half that they'd already spent playing and recording as Korn seemed to have gone by in the blink of an eye. The poverty, the dead-end jobs, the mac-and-cheese dinners . . . all were forgotten. As Munky explained, "We wrote these songs, got signed, and then the tour bus pulled up in front of our house. We haven't looked back since."

5

the road warrior's booty

Shipments of *Korn* were to be delivered to record stores across America on October 4, 1994. With no scheduled press conferences, little critical attention, and even less advertising to trumpet their arrival, the boxes of CDs were not expected to sell out anytime in the foreseeable future. Then again, no one, least of all the men of Korn, had ever pinned any hopes on an overnight success story. Our assiduous heroes were just happy to be on tour.

The last time they'd taken to the nation's highways and byways, it had been as an unsigned act. Like so many start-up bands, they'd had to purchase a dilapidated RV, cart their gear about the California coast in a rattletrap trailer hook-up, shower at truck stops, and pray for a decent turnout. According to Munky, some of those first gigs saw Korn playing to "crowds" of only four or five people—"and we're like, 'And our next song, Mom, is . . .'" No doubt, the tour bus and the built-in audiences of Biohazard and House of Pain came as a welcome change of pace. Better yet, the group actually had enough of a repertoire to draw up some solid set lists.

Perhaps the most beneficial aspect of the touring was that it finally provided Jonathan with an incentive strong enough to break his two-year crank habit. "Oh, I loved it," he said of the tour. "When we first got on the road it was with House of Pain, and I had to come off speed." Although plenty of musicians have been known to juggle the responsibilities of feeding their addiction with those of live performance, it's important to remember that Jonathan had already "stayed up for two years straight."

Battling a drug problem while staging an extensive tour is a no-win proposition. If the first doesn't get you, then the other one will, so to speak. Jonathan was convinced that if he kept awake through the grueling tour, he would not live to see the end of it. And rightly so, for Korn's first national outing was not bound to be just any old tour. The road trip would span a total of eighteen months, and all respites would be kept to a bare minimum. Even Jonathan's hyperdeveloped death instinct wasn't as dominant as all that.

The band has always operated under the "extra mile" principle. If the record consumers aren't biting, tour longer. If the audience isn't digging your act, try harder. No doubt, much of this renowned work ethic was acquired in the final months of 1994, as the unknown quintet toured in support of their forthcoming debut.

Another hardcore thrash-metal—or whatever the hell you wanna call it—outfit might have taken a dim view of playing to hip-hop audiences, but Korn were undeterred. If people didn't love them from the outset, they would seduce them through sheer force of will. "We'll go out if nobody's heard of us and we'll just, we'll push harder and make 'em like us," Fieldy affirmed. "That's all you gotta do."

The surge of adrenaline that accompanied each performance endowed the guys with supernatural strength. Their shows positively oozed with infectious energy. People who'd never even heard of the band would forget all about trying to save their strength for the headliners' rendition of "Jump Around," and take to their feet. For the instigators of the mayhem, the sight of moshing bodies drenched in sweat was the essence of success.

As predicted, it was not with a roar but with a whimper that *Korn* finally reached retail outlets on October 4. "When the first record came out, we hoped that it would slowly build a following," Jonathan said. "And for the first six months after it came out, the key word was definitely 'slow.' It really wasn't selling at all."

The few that did buy the CD, however, found that whatever *Korn* may have lacked in promotional flash, it made up for in explosive substance. From the wake-up call sounded by the first discordant guitar riffs, to the guttural, *"Are you readyyy?"* that seemed to come from the very depths of the ninth circle, to the bass-heavy tone that ran the length of the album, *Korn* was like nothing anyone had ever heard. Listening to the album for the first time is as hypnotically traumatic an experience as staring down the barrel of a .44-caliber.

And the gut-wrenching groove just never lets up. Instead, the intensity crescendos, peaking with Jonathan raging, *"You can suck my dick and fuckin' like it!"* in the middle of "Faget." Finally, just when one thinks they can stand it no longer, the CD's nerve-racking progress ends in the manner of all successful therapy sessions—uncontrollable sobbing.

Much like the *Korn* cover photo, where an ominous male figure casts a dark shadow over the bright, young playground-goer, the collection of songs, taken together, provides the perfect prescription for sunny-day despair. The album promised to become the quintessential soundtrack for troubled and rebellious youth worldwide. Korn and Immortal Records knew they had a winner. But due to an underwhelming response from mainstream media outlets, citizens of the world-at-large had nary a clue. Only the rare reviewer took the time to really hear the music. Apparently, *Huh* magazine boasted just such a reviewer. "Angry, aggro, and crazed, Korn's debut isn't just some of the most intense metal since Metallica's *Master of Puppets*, it also has a confrontational vibe that Pantera tries (and fails) to achieve," the critic wrote. "With a thickness in both the guitars and rhythms, these tunes lock into a tight groove like the tumblers of a safe bank."

The positive feedback was an ego boost to be sure, but no way was *Huh* going to sway hundreds of thousands of record-buyers. Only Korn themselves could do that. "We had the cards stacked against us when our first album came out, with this kind of music," Jonathan explained. "Everybody was scared of it . . . So from the start we were fighting that battle, and the record label knew they were gonna have to invest in us and put us on the road 'cause that's the only way we were gonna get out there: by constant touring."

The radio stations' collective response to "Blind" had been one of unmitigated hostility. Many informed Korn's promoters that "it would be a cold day in hell" before they played the single. MTV was hardly more receptive. Korn would dutifully submit their videos for "Blind," "Shoots and Ladders," and "Clown," but according to David, "MTV always forgot about them or they simply didn't like our sound, they never got shown." The group was left with no choice but to go it the old-fashioned way. "We just started playing and playing," David continued, "doing gig after gig and support after support."

Long after House of Pain and Biohazard had grown road-weary, Korn's bus just kept on rolling. Sick of It All, Orange 9mm, Primus, 311, Fear Factory, Danzig, Marilyn Manson, Megadeth, Monster Magnet, KMFDM, Cypress Hill, Life of Agony, Ozzy Osbourne—in the quest for fans and attention, Korn would open for them all. "We went out for eighteen months straight," Jonathan said. "I think we played 380 shows a year, and there's only 365 days. That's what you've got to do. You've got to work hard to be successful."

Stocked with an arsenal of alcohol that would put Liquor Mart to shame and enough porno mags to fill an adult bookstore, the tour bus had all the makings of home. Five narrow bunks, a small lounge area and a CD collection featuring the Village People and Blondie completed the picture of domestic bliss. If the quintet could only stand the oppressive heat that often beset their well-equipped rider, maybe they'd live to headline an arena of their own.

It became obvious right from the start that the infamous concert-tour experience would be more *Road Rules* than *Behind the Music*. Sex and drugs had given way to serious girlfriends and Narcotics Anonymous brochures. Jonathan's sizable HIV tattoo served as a steadfast red flag, checking the vocalist's baser instincts at every turn. "I thought touring would be one big-ass fucking party—chicks everywhere, the whole fantasy," he recalled. "It's nothing like I thought. It's better. If it was like what I thought it would be, I'd be dead now."

None of which is to say that the band wholly abstained from the vices of a wine, women, and song lifestyle. Drinking was elevated to an art form on that moving wet bar of a tour bus. In this respect, Jonathan was especially wanton. Something had to take the place of his speed habit and help him sleep after the intense shows. "I'd walk around and drink a whole big liter bottle [of Jägermeister] every night," he said. "Fuck, I'd drink a whole bottle in a night. Everybody else would be walking around swigging from beer bottles, and I'd be doing the same thing, walking around with a Jägermeister."

The swill also came in handy before the concerts. Shifting from the laid-back vibe of the bus to the stage-stomping ferocity of their live act was a maneuver that required some reinforcement. "Yeah, that's why we drink so much. It helps us," reasoned Fieldy. "I guess that's part of the deal, it's part of the show. I mean, it's not as emotional as it is, like, in the studio. Live, it's more intense, it's like when you are onstage for an hour and ten minutes, it's like being on a roller coaster for an hour and ten minutes. It's just intense the whole time, sometimes I'll be walkin' offstage and I'll be like throwin' up—I'm throwin' up a couple of times onstage, too. It's just because it's so intense being up there. Sometimes I will be throwin' up before we play, too."

As anyone who's seen a Korn show knows, the band's crazed onstage demeanor requires a full commitment. This is not the type of music one could simply execute, it has to come straight from the gut. Munky found that the shows unleashed his inner demons. If there was any quality he didn't like about himself, chances were he'd come face-to-face with it onstage. The band's frontman would effect a similar transformation. The pain and emotion of his lyrics required that he immerse himself completely. If he broke concentration midshow, as he did on a couple of occasions, the whole performance was as good as over. In his opinion, he'd ruined it.

Such was no doubt the case the one time that Korn tried to reenact "Daddy" in concert. The paroxysm of weeping that tops off the CD version had happened with absolutely no forethought on Jonathan's part. Neither did he give much consideration to the effect that the song would have in live performance. Apparently, whatever it was, he thought he could handle it when the band agreed to include the track at a New York club date. Big mistake. "It fucked me up bad," said Jonathan. To this day, he refuses to so much as listen to the distressing song, much less perform it.

Of course, when it came to ensuring the success of every tour date, Jonathan did not stop at excluding "Daddy" from the playlists. According to Munky, the pied bagpiper went to far greater lengths for his art. "Jonathan will sit there before we go onstage and take himself to this place he hates," Munky said. "It's really scary to watch. We feed off his energy and give it back to him. It's like we're directing our own scary movie."

For his part, Jonathan denies giving his band the pre-show willies. He does, however, freely admit that after the last set, it's open season on anyone who dares speak to him before he's fully recovered. "I have a cool-down period where I have to get people the fuck away from me or I'll freak," he warned. "It takes me about fifteen or twenty minutes to come down, then I'm just fine. Like before I go on, I'm normal until I hit the stage, then *boom*, it kicks in. Then after, it takes me a while to wind down. I freak the fuck out when I get off the stage."

Night after vital-fluid–sapping night, the band would shred their stage to smithereens. An attack of unstoppable momentum beginning to end, the shows were a testament to Korn's sheer staying power. The braying of Jonathan's bagpipes never failed to shock even the harshest audiences into a moment of stunned submission. You only needed one good eardrum to discern that these guys were out for moshers' blood, and nine out of ten people appreciated both the action-packed performance and the authentic sentiment behind it. Walking toward their cars with the sound of "Faget" or "Blind" running through their minds, the newly initiated were determined to make this off-kilter metal band with the modern, heavy groove a permanent part of their CD collections.

———

Within a few months of the tour's inception, sales of *Korn* showed a marked increase. The up-close-and-personal approach was working like a charm. By the time Korn headed out with Ozzy Osbourne in the winter of 1996, their album was selling at the rate of 17,000 per week. While the guys would call their management office every Wednesday morning to check on the latest sales figures, they need only have looked to the changing face of their fan base to observe their ever-growing clout.

In the year and a half they'd been on the road, Korn had seen every conceivable brand of audience—the long-hairs and the mulletheads, the white face-powder–and–black hair-dye set, and, of course, the plywood-surfers' faction. Apparently, the band's hybrid sound had something for everyone. "We've got metal fans, alternative fans, Goth fans, punk fans, and hardcore kids," boasted Jonathan. "You go to one of our headlining shows, you see all kinds of people. I like that. It shows that kids don't listen to us because it's cool." In this instance, the frontman didn't speak for the entire band. Fieldy expressed far less enthusiastic sentiments, saying, "I remember calling my girlfriend a couple of times and saying like, 'You should see this crowd.' I don't know, man, it was like they were out of the eighties."

In time, a Korn concert uniform would indeed emerge. The kids would show up dressed in logo-emblazoned T-shirts, Adidas track suits, and meticulously braided coifs à la Brian; but in the spring of '95, when Korn took the stage to warm up thousands of Danzig fans, that day was still a year or so in the coming. And yet it was already clear that the guys were beginning to make a real name for themselves. People had actually turned out early to catch the little-known opening act with the great word of mouth. As the musicians looked out at the chaotic sea of faces crowding the auditorium, they knew this tour could really push them over the edge.

On the heels of the Danzig tour, Korn proceeded to open for Marilyn Manson. Again, the vast crowd of spectators motivated the band to try and outdo the headlining act. After the shows, Korn would put their young-band Napoleonic complex aside to bond with the main attractions. The spooky kids of Marilyn Manson proved the ideal tourmates. Within a few days, the groups were discussing the finer points of Satanism, painting the towns, and (mis)behaving as though they'd been sharing a stage for years. "They're great," enthused Jonathan. "Manson are my buddies. I love hanging out with those guys. Every time we go out, we get in trouble. Just nutty, crazy shit." As we shall soon see, these warm words notwithstanding, the friendship between Korn and Marilyn Manson would not endure the test of time.

Another indication of Korn's impending notoriety came when they played a supporting role on Megadeth's bill in the summer of '95. While the audience response was mixed—with some of the die-hard dirtheads throwing everything but the kitchen sink at our heroes—many in attendance did choose to beat a hasty retreat right after Korn's show. Still, the Megadeth experience proved wanting in several categories: If the dodging of bottles and cans wasn't bad enough, the group was also confronted by Dave Mustaine's larger-than-life attitude problem. According to Brian, Megadeth's guitar-playing frontman was a consummate "dick."

Jonathan agreed with Brian's indictment, saying that "the other Mega-guys were cool; it was that Dave guy. There were all these rules. We almost got kicked off the tour for throwing some water at the crowd. It was ridiculous."

The most ludicrous scene of all took place shortly before one of the concerts. Mustaine, who'd been doing battle with the bottle ever since his drug habit had got him kicked out of Metallica back in the early 1980s, came aboard the Korn mobile, drunk as a prom queen.

"What now?" thought the beleaguered members of Korn.

Clearly looking to throw his weight around, Mustaine scanned the bus to ensure the presence of a captive audience.

"Do you know what you need to do to get big?" he began, slurring his speech and wagging his finger.

Before anyone had a chance to respond, he furnished his own answer. "Only tour with big bands."

Now, here was a real lesson for the guys of Korn. At tour's end, they were free to tell the press, and anyone else who cared to listen, that thanks to Megadeth, they'd "learned how *not* to treat the opening band."

Toward the end of the summer, the quintet was only too ready to hop a plane for Europe. They didn't intend to stay long, just long enough to start people talking about the belated release of *Korn*. Although the LP wasn't scheduled to arrive until November 1995, a few U.K. publications had already taken to championing Korn's cause. Leading the pack were the prescient editors of *Mörat Kerrang!*, who arranged to interview and photograph the band upon hearing of their arrival. No sooner had the album been released, than they ran the article; the headline read: "Californian mob Korn might just be the next big thing . . ."

After putting in a surprise appearance to open for Primus, and headlining a sold-out show at London's LA2 club, Korn headed for the Continent to play with German industrialists KMFDM. Once they crossed the Channel, the brief tour took a turn for the unpleasant. Having tried and failed to get across the Atlantic back in their LAPD days, the band was surprised to find that Europe was not all it was cracked up to be. "It fuckin' sucks," said Jonathan. "We had a bad fuckin' experience in Germany, where some fucker tried to throw us out of a restaurant 'cause we were fuckin' American. The only places that were cool were London and Manchester—the English-speaking places. And Amsterdam [as well]—Holland's cool. Other than that, it was really fucked-up. We had really fucked-up tour managers, and we'd be sitting in our hotel rooms not knowing what to do. So we had a really fucked-up time. And we didn't know any other bands—they stick to themselves mostly over there—so it was really fucked-up for us."

No doubt, much of Holland's allure could be attributed to the country's laid-back stance on the hashish question, and its exotic and readily available pornography. As indicated by the artwork on the inside flap of the *Korn* CD cover, this is a group that takes the adult-entertainment industry very seriously. The wares boasted by Amsterdam's XXX-purveyors made even Korn's favorite rags look well-nigh tasteful in comparison. This was the opportunity of a lifetime. Like kids at a Halloween-night candy store free-for-all, they stuffed their duffel bags full of publications such as *Animal Orgy*, and headed back to the States . . . five obscenely satisfied customers.

Even as Korn's bus was burning rubber down the auto-bahn, Jonathan's mind was consumed by thoughts of the girlfriend who was waiting for him back in Long Beach, California. His feelings for her ran deep, and vice versa. Renée Perez had once made great sacrifices to keep her boyfriend in beer and track suits. According to Jonathan, it hadn't been easy. "I love my girlfriend now, because I trust her and she's been with me since I was nothing," he stated. "She lived with me in a fucking closet in my house, she borrowed money from her parents to keep me and pay our rent, she believed in me. Now, if I met some girl, it would be different, I would always have that thing in the back of my mind that she's with me because of who I am."

While Jon and Renée had no immediate plans to marry, the couple was with child. When the band returned to the U.S., the singer's girlfriend was already well into her third trimester. And with *Korn* fast approaching the 500,000 gold-record mark, Jonathan was turning into quite the breadwinner. Eventually, David, Fieldy, and Head would take their frontman's cue and start families of their own. In the meantime, however, Jonathan was the only one with breast-feeding and ob/gyns on the brain.

While the band never quit touring, the vocalist carried a beeper on his person at all times—"This tells me when my child's coming. If I'm onstage, I say: 'I'm having a baby now, 'bye!' " To ascertain the sex of his would-be baby, he also sought out the same Bakersfield psychic who had predicted his rise to rock stardom. "My astrologer told me it was going to be a girl," he related. "My little girl has been coming to me in my dreams, and it's breaking my fucking heart."

Jonathan was planning to name his daughter Salaam Dementia, when Renée gave birth to a bouncing baby boy on October 18, 1995. So much for ten-dollar prophecies. And yet Jonathan couldn't have cared less—girl or boy, all that mattered was that he was now a father. "All I know is, when I had a kid and I stared down at him, something happened to me. I thought, 'This is why I'm here—to pass myself on to another little human being.' Somehow, that makes sense to me. You grow up, you have kids, you die, and a piece of you goes on . . . Watching my kid being born was the most beautiful thing I ever saw."

Jonathan and his girlfriend named their son Nathan Houseman and Korn carried on the same as before—save, perhaps, for one modest alteration. Fatherhood had started Jonathan thinking about cleaning up his hard-drinking lifestyle. But laying off the Jäger bottle would not be easy, as the liquor company was providing Korn with free product and a bevy of scantily clad Jägerettes (think Hooter's girls bearing Jägermeister). Finally Jonathan had to put his foot down. He asked that the Jäger be taken off the rider, and "restricted" himself to fifteen glasses of Jack and Coke per night.

A few weeks after Nathan was born, Korn pointed their tour bus for home. They'd already been on the road for over a year and criss-crossed the U.S. some three times in the process. The travels had seen the group form lasting connections with a variety of musical acts. Northern California's Deftones, for one, were now Korn's "brother band." Not only did they share Jonathan's affinity for Duran Duran, recording a cover of his favorite song "The Chauffeur," but their performances with Korn never failed to inspire total mayhem.

The young Aussies of Silverchair had also become great fans, going so far as to affix Korn stickers to their onstage accoutrements. Whenever David and Jonathan would run into the underaged rockers, they would invariably attempt to ply them with drink. But since Silverchair never ventured far outside the watchful gaze of their parents, all such efforts amounted to naught.

Two of Korn's favorite hard-rock outfits, Sepultura and Machine Head, had come out as vociferous supporters of the Korn sound early on. Considering the silence of the mainstream press, the praise of their fellow musicmen gratified the band to no end. "Musicians are the hardest people to satisfy," explained Jonathan, "so when someone like Robb [Flynn of Machine Head] gives you a compliment, it's the best." Sepultura had also shown amazing foresight by trying to appropriate Korn's sonic stylings before the band had actually broken. They'd even hired Ross Robinson to produce their forthcoming album, *Roots*, and then proceeded to schedule studio time at Indigo Ranch. The adulation inspired the members of Korn with a mixed bag of feelings. Even Jonathan, who'd put in a cameo appearance on the Sepultura LP, had a hard time overcoming his initial ambivalence. "I was shocked when they got our producer and recorded it here," he said. "It was blatant, but it was also so flattering. Sepultura are one of my favorite heavy bands and I feel honored by it."

While chasing the fame that was just barely outside their grasp, Korn found themselves passing through Jacksonville, Florida. It was there they came upon one über-resourceful and highly crafty fan who made no secret of his admiration. His name was Fred Durst, and—wouldn't you know it?—he also had a rock band. At the time, Limp Bizkit wasn't so much as a year old. But, then again, the Bizkit's fearless leader has never been the sort to let a golden opportunity slip through his fingers.

Having spotted Fieldy and Head loitering about their tour bus, he presented his tattoo artist's creds and offered to ink the band after their show. "Fred told us he'd been tattooing for years," recalled Jonathan. "But it turned out it was, like, his third tattoo! He did a KOᴙN tattoo on Head's back—and it looked like HoᴙN." Instead of filing a malpractice suit, Head and Fieldy agreed to give Durst's band a fair hearing. When Limp Bizkit's demo tape arrived at Fieldy's home a few months hence, the bass man was quick to send it to Korn's management. "And the next thing you know, all these labels were calling," recalled a very rich and happy Fred Durst.

Outside of the music industry, esteem for the band was

on the rise as well. By Christmas 1995, Korn were a certified underground sensation. While their videos and singles were still going unnoticed by media outlets nationwide, the kids who'd formerly turned a deaf ear to hard rock—choosing instead to follow the ongoing saga of the East and West Coast rappers—had at length begun to rediscover the virtues of the dissonant guitar and anguished vocals. Jonathan found himself besieged by fans who could relate to his lyrics only too well. Whether they'd been mistreated by parents, molested by relatives, or taunted at school, teens from all walks of life wanted to let Korn know that their songs had saved them from the clutches of suicidal despair.

Of course, one can't expect to please all the people all of the time. It was also during this first year of touring that the infamous feud between Korn and their sometime headliner Fear Factory first began to rage. What sparked the mutual animosity is uncertain, but there's no doubt about the fact that Fear Factory's Dino Cazares had charged Korn with "ripping off" his band. These were fighting words, and our protagonists were ready to rumble. "I hate that jealous bitch," Jonathan retorted. "I heard [Cazares] just got a seven-string guitar like us and he's wearing Adidas suits like me. I don't understand it." The ill will between the bands would continue, and was even rumored to have escalated into full-blown physical combat on at least one occasion.

Back in the last weeks of 1995, however, fisticuffs were the last thing on the band's mind. The upcoming holidays, the newborn baby, and the sheer physical exhaustion of fourteen months on the road conspired to bring Korn's wandering ways to a temporary end. The guys went home to see their girlfriends and their families, not to perform again until 1996.

The three weeks of vacation time went by like a ten-minute break in the middle of one of those antiquated, forty-eight-hour dance marathons. No sooner had the band embarked upon their regimen of peace and quiet, than they were startled out of their reverie by the ringing in of the new year. Before they knew it, Fieldy, Munky, Brian, Jonathan, and David were once again packing their bags and saying their good-byes.

On this particular outing, however, the band had the consolation of knowing that they'd be traveling in high style. Having snagged the coveted opening-act position on Ozzy Osbourne's triumphant "Retirement Sucks" tour, Korn would be playing for tens of thousands of people each time they took the stage. Better still, they'd actually get a few days off to compose some new songs this time out. The group had had neither the time nor the inclination to sit down and write since they'd recorded their album some eighteen months ago. But with their scope of influence spreading at an exponential rate, more and more people were chomping at the bit for another record. Suddenly, Korn was a high-stakes venture, and the band was beginning to feel the pressure.

After arranging to set up a studio on their tour bus, the guys were ready to celebrate this latest coup. Not only was this tour certain to do wonders for their ever-proliferating fan base, but they'd be opening up for Ozzy Osbourne, the alpha male of heavy metal, and their all-time hero. Although the Black Sabbath experience had not featured prominently in Jonathan's formative years, he could appreciate the magnitude of his band's latest achievement. "The rest of my band [are fans]. Some of them were fuckin' Ozzy for Halloween. They're stoked to go out with 'The Man.' I'm stoked, too. I respect him immensely. And he's all clean now."

The same could not be said for Jonathan Davis. Although he'd gone out of his way to avoid Jägermeister, and had hardly touched a drop of liquor during his twenty-day rest period, all bets were off when his twenty-fifth birthday rolled around. On January 17, Jonathan was hanging out at Manhattan's Whiskey Bar with a roadie and Ozzy's drummer. At the stroke of midnight, he began to drink like a man possessed. Using Jack and Coke as a chaser, he downed fifteen shots of Jäger. Who knows how much more he could have guzzled, had gravity not intervened. The drinking binge ended with Jonathan toppling off his bar stool and stabbing his face with a burning cigarette (which, incidentally, he continued to smoke as he lay prostrate on the floor). Feeling no pain, Jonathan still had the presence of mind to return to his hotel room, where he proceeded to pass out cold.

The next day, Korn was supposed to open for Ozzy at Meadowlands. "I woke up in the morning and I was so fuckin' hungover," recalled Jonathan. "I was getting out of the bus and I fainted. They had to get two people to carry me in. They dragged me in, like right in front of Ozzy and Sharon, his wife, everybody. Just looking like, fucked-up! I go to the stage, I faint again. They slapped me, threw me onstage and I pulled the show off. I don't know how the hell I did it. I didn't know what words were coming next, I didn't know what song it was. I just fuckin' closed my eyes. I'd been doing it for so long, I pulled it off."

But Jonathan isn't the only one who came away from the Retirement Sucks tour with a tale of public humiliation. While supporting Ozzy at the L.A. Forum, Fieldy had his own brush with shame. Going all-out to give the heavy-metal audience the headbanging experience they'd come out for, the bassman was thrashing about like a hopped-up dervish, jumping atop monitors and quite literally putting life and limb on the line. Somewhere in the middle of all this madness, he took a wrong step and found himself lying facedown on his broken bass.

The twenty thousand witnesses who'd watched him bite the stage were suddenly on their feet, cheering. Although Fieldy had given the ticketholders their money's worth, this would no doubt go down as one of the more embarrassing incidents of his career. "It was like, 'Oh my God.' I don't think you can really embarrass yourself more than in front of twenty thousand people," he attested. "If you're going to make an ass of yourself, I guess that's the best way to do it."

Getting a rise out of a crowd of Ozzyphiles was an accomplishment all in itself. So what if it had taken a splintered bass to do it? Every time that Korn had hit the concert trail with a big-name metal act, they'd had to bust out all their moves just to keep the natives from growing restless and lynching their hip-hop-influenced arses. Their high-octane performances had gone off with varying degrees of success, but at year's end, Korn had come through their extended baptism-by-fire with their dreams intact.

By the time the band set out to conquer the U.S. with Ozzy, MTV and radio had already begun to devote some off-off-peak airtime to "Blind," music magazines were paying close attention, and they were *this close* to a gold record. For all this bounty, the band had no one but themselves to thank. The crusades of the last year had taxed their every faculty—spirit, mind, and liver. And yet, *Korn* had yet to find the all-important 500,000 buyers. "We want it to go gold, and go out and headline our own U.S. tour," David had explained a few months before the Ozzy trek.

Given its middling performance on the *Billboard* charts, Korn-watchers were shocked when the CD finally hit the mark in January of 1996. The guys were in a bar, conducting a soundcheck, when their manager called with the monumental news flash. Having worked so hard and sacrificed so much for the acceptance that a gold record symbolized, Fieldy, Munky, Brian, and David immediately set about calling their families and friends. With every new person they told, they felt as if they were experiencing the joy of the occasion afresh. "It was so cool! We called our parents, and all the people that supported us from the beginning, and told them. That was the best part," affirmed David. "But it's not like, 'We made it . . . We got a gold record.' It is a success, I guess, and it's cool. But it's not that big of a deal. It's something to hang on your wall."

Jonathan was of a different opinion. "Jon is the only one who is really crazy about it," David continued. "When our manager called us and told us about it . . . he broke down in tears." Having exposed his very soul to the world, the public's reaction meant everything. To him, the plaque was the Golden Fleece *and* the Holy Grail. It had been the be-all and end-all of his existence ever since Korn had signed with Immortal. And inasmuch as the realization of this long-held dream ushered in a new era for the band, it also signaled the end of their collective childhood. Many more goals would be fulfilled, milestones met, and personal records broken, but the memory of their very first conquest would remain with the band forever.

6
bumper krop

On January 29, 1996, the day that the gold certification was bestowed upon *Korn*, pedestrians went along their merry ways, blissfully ignorant of both the celebratory mood that pervaded Korn's hotel room, and the effect that the band's largely unsung achievement would soon have on their favorite alt-rock radio stations.

That night, the five gold-selling artists had a mind to party, as did their crew of roadies, sound personnel, and various faces from the Ozzy camp. The man/myth/legend was also in attendance, having taken it upon himself to present the band with a token of his esteem. "[Ozzy]'s a really, really, really cool guy," enthused Jonathan. "When we got our gold album, he came in and wheeled in this cart of booze, like all sorts of beer and champagne, and said congratulations and hung out with us in our room . . . Really, experiences like that make it all worthwhile. In fact, there really have been no low points. It's been all high points. All of us are fulfilling our dreams doing this, and we're getting to see the world and play for all these people. I mean, how can you question that? There can't be low points."

True enough, the climb up the grid chart of success had been as inordinately steady as it had been painfully slow.

But just as the band's ground zero now lay a long ways behind them, their ultimate peak was still nowhere in sight. At this point of no return, no one—not the MOR-loving masses, not the growing army of Korn fans, not even the band members themselves—could have surmised that the Bakersfield Five would one day raze the face of the sonic landscape as we knew it.

For a band that had never expected much in the way of commercial success, nor aimed for a sound with mass appeal, 500,000 albums was a staggering sum. They could only hope that their next public offering did as well—at least, that's what one would have assumed. But Korn had extended their "more is more" mentality to every facet of their professional lives. One goal automatically begot another, and these guys were not going to stop until complete and total world domination was theirs.

And therein lay the quandary. The group's immense mass of fans demanded an encore and, for all their well-laid plans, the band had yet to come up with a bass line, a riff, or lyric. Now, in the first bloom of youth, Korn had no time to spare. They had to capitalize on the momentum immediately, before people grew weary of listening to the same twelve songs. In March 1996, when the Ozzy tour came to its conclusion, Korn's record label and management team took a hard look at the figures—all told, 600,000 units sold, and still counting—rubbed their eyes in utter disbelief, and applied the massive pressure tactics.

"You gotta get this album out," the record company urged.

"It's imperative to your career," said management.

"I think that people were afraid that the intensity of the first album would go away too quickly," Munky explained. "We kind of already had a buzz and wanted to stay out there and stay in the public's face."

While the band understood the urgency of their situation, touring had sapped every creative impulse, and the hand of inspiration could not be forced. After Ozzy's extravaganza, they needed a long spell of R&R. A month, however, was all the recovery time they could afford. Since the album had to go out in October, exactly two years after *Korn*'s release, the band would have to write and record with all due haste if they wanted to meet their deadline.

Adding to the band's escalating anxiety were the whispers of "the sophomore curse" and "one-hit wonders." Once again, the guys got the sinking feeling that they would have to prove themselves anew. And this time, they wouldn't have the luxury of time to fall back on. "When you're a little baby band, the first album's always good, because you had all your life to write those songs," Jonathan explained. "But the second album—you come off the road and you've got to get this album done, and then you've got to get right back out on the road."

In the midst of this crunch, the group managed to keep it together. They sensed that the light of inspiration would not fail to shine once they got into the rehearsal studio that May. Of course, given all the undue strain, they couldn't have been too sure.

Signs that Korn was inching toward the mainstream had been few and far between. Aside from the none-too-overt MTV and radio exposure, the waxing interest of the fringe print media, and the gold record, there had been little evidence to suggest that this quintet was indeed the Next Big Thing. Before heading into the studio, though, the band would subtract two more claims to underground status from their list.

Big-budget feature films have long had a way of raising the profile of little-known bands. So much so, that appearing on a soundtrack has come to denote a bid for mass acceptance. Much as the Offspring's inclusion on 1992's *The Chase* soundtrack had alerted the subterranean fan base of the punk band's impending defection, so did Korn's turn on the *The Crow: City of Angels* CD start many of the fans who'd gotten in on the ground floor worrying about the commodification of their favorite vegetable.

"We built such a big following, and such demand came around, since we've been all around the States about five times, that we were pretty much forced into that mainstream thing by the kids," Jonathan reasoned. "Requesting it on the radio, wanting to read articles on us—all the kids want us, so people start jumping on it. It's all the kids, but what's really funny is when you get that mainstream success, people start bagging on you for it. And it's not really your fault. We're on a lot of radio now. It's crazy, I never, ever thought this would happen. It's pretty cool, though."

Clearly, the dissatisfied grumbling of the first-comers could not dissuade Jonathan from following the open road to the forefront of the music industry. As for Munky, Brian, Fieldy, and David, they still believed that they *were* underground. After all, it wasn't as if they'd ever pandered to the masses. Following the golden rule of "Do unto others as you would have done unto you," they recorded only the kind of music they would want to hear—it was that simple.

Since the sequel to the wildly popular *The Crow* was certain to include a soundtrack to rival the industrial intensity of its predecessor, the group saw no conflict between their hardcore integrity and career objectives. So they wrote and recorded a song for the movie, naming it "Sean Olson," after their friend of the same name. Not much ado would be made of this contribution upon the CD's July 1996 release, but in a year's time, Korn would catch some flack from across the Atlantic, where the song was released as part of an EP. Even the normally liberal Europeans, it seemed, had a hard time stomaching Korn. "In Europe there's some shit with 'Sean Olson' . . . because of the end where I scream, *'I'm cumming, I'm cumming, I'm cumming on you'* . . . they take me too literally or something," griped Jonathan. "That song really is about being fucked over by friends, or so-called friends, and getting them back in the end."

Foreshadowing of imminent breakage also came in the form of a nod from the KISS reunion tour. Shortly after signing off the Ozzy show, Korn were invited to open for the supergroup's Los Angeles concert. Like the rest of America, Korn had given up the pyrotechnically-gifted seventies rockers for retired. On the night of the show, however, tens of thousands of fans crowded the arena, screaming for KISS. In the midst of all the excitement, Korn forgot all about their motto to "try and be better than the leading act," and concentrated on having a great time. According to Jonathan, the night turned into one of the most memorable performances of his career to date. "To open for them was incredible," he said, "because I just never thought I'd ever see them in concert . . . it was nutty, it was crazy . . . Opening for them was cool."

And on that note, the wild ride had ended. Finales didn't come any grander and blazes of glory didn't flare any brighter. But even as the curtain dropped on act one of *The Story of Korn*, and audiences filed out for intermission, the band was already setting the stage for act two.

7

let 'em eat korn

In May 1996, Korn were faced with the unenviable task of writing and recording their crucial follow-up album under a four-month deadline. Although they'd taken April off to convalesce, the guys were still reeling from their fourteen months of kamikaze touring. Disoriented and not-a-little-bit confused by their increasing importance to the label and to their fans, they entered the studio prepared to make the best of an unsavory situation.

Dismissing their fears, and focusing instead on their zest for writing and studio work, they psyched themselves up for the four solid months of work that lay ahead. As Jonathan explained, "We don't plan on being a one-hit wonder. Our next album will be Korn. We would have grown and learned some things, but we still will be Korn." In another interview, the singer promised that the album would be "a little bit different. Lyrically, I know that I'll try some different stuff, but it'll still be the same old Korn. I don't want it to change too drastically [from our first album]. Just basically stay with what we've been doing, but change it a little bit—add some flavor to it."

While the band had not written a lick for two years running, they'd grown stronger by dint of ceaseless touring. Sounding better and tighter than ever before, they embarked upon pre-production determined to make good on their assurances to the fans. Sure enough, the lightning pace of the writing sessions was reminiscent of the time they'd recorded their demo. The songwriting came so naturally that Munky had to attribute the phenomenon to "a lot of creativity buildup, like blue balls of creativity. In the studio it just kinda spewed out."

Six days a week, the five musicians would meet in the studio and enter the creative zone, not to part company until some ten hours had passed and at least one song had been written. With only a month at their disposal, every minute counted. Although the time restriction made Korn's democratic decision-making process difficult to maintain, Brian insisted that "nothing gets past any band member without his approval. None of us are afraid to tell the other guy, 'That sucks.' We get over it. It might hurt for a while, but at least we know no one's going to be hating it when we play the same song every night."

Once again, Fieldy took the lead in songwriting and Ross Robinson presided over every rehearsal. With five self-absorbed musicians working out chords in one room, Ross's presence was invaluable. Many was the time that the producer or, as the guys affectionately called him, "the cheerleader," had to step in to keep a good riff from going to waste. "Somebody plays something and no one says nothin'—everybody's too lazy," Fieldy admitted. "[Munky] could play something cool and it'll just go straight past 'cause we're too busy being arrogant with ourselves. I'll be busy playing my stuff, I won't even hear what he's doing. We have to have somebody to point it out like, 'What are you playing over there?' . . . All kinds of riffs go past that might be good that we just don't hear 'cause anything we play we don't think is good, somebody has to tell us, you know, like, 'What was that?' "

From there on out, it was just a matter of bringing all the elements together. Always building on a riff, the band would experiment with every imaginable aural sensation until they had molded a song that would do their distinguished name justice. Providing suggestions and feedback, Jonathan waited until the arrangements were complete to put his lyricist's skills to the test. And make no mistake, this was in fact a test. As the vocalist had relied upon the kindness of crank to write the first album, there were no guarantees that he'd be able to repeat the stand-out performance without his trusty little helper.

Confining himself to a commodious room in Hollywood's Magic Hotel, Jonathan began his five-day writing spree by chugging half a bottle of Jäger. Looking out the window onto the city sprawled out beneath, he was suddenly seized by a fit of ideas. Right there and then, he wrote five full songs. "They just come to me. It's weird. It's not like I have to sit there and screw with it. It just came out, *bam!* It comes in spurts and then I'm sitting there for another day looking at a piece of paper, and then *bam!* It's another five songs. But this one's definitely more mature. The last one, I just had a bunch of things I had to get out from since I was a little kid. This one's dealing more with now, all that time being on the road for a year and a half. There's some strange ones."

"Strange" was a well-chosen word, given titles like "Chi," "Mr. Rogers," "K@#%!," "A.D.I.D.A.S.," and "Ass Itch." Oddly enough, it was the track with the most traditional title that turned out to be the most bizarre. Despite a myriad of Internet-inspired rumors to the contrary, "Twist" was a barrage of indecipherable blather from start to finish, with the exception of one word, "twist." Although Jonathan has affirmed as much, fans would have their say. Proving once again that Web masters can decode any language, one Web site translated the song's lyrics as . . .

YOUR NOT RAT DAT NOT THEN THEY PUSH STOP IT
  TAKE A
MINUTE, RAT TUT, TAKE A MOB AT THAT THEN I
  PICK UP A
ROCK SO THEN I PRETEND TO PICK UP A BAT, ROCK
SOMETHING IN MY HEART, IT DONT MATTER I
  REMEMBER
ROCKS, SOMETHING, RUNNING IN MA I HIT THE BONE
  I THINK
WHY IS IT SO? ROCK SAID I DO NOT EGZAGERATE
  OVER IT NOW
GETTING UP BUT I RUN NOTHING BUT A ROCK
TWIST TWIST TWIST

YOUR NOT RAT DAT NOT THEN THEY PUSH STOP IT
  TAKE A
MINUTE, RAT TUT, TAKE A MOB AT THAT THEN I
  PICK UP A
ROCK SO THEN I PRETEND TO PICK UP A BAT, ROCK
SOMETHING IN MY HEART, IT DONT MATTER I
  REMEMBER
ROCKS, SOMETHING, RUNNING IN MA I HIT THE BONE
  I THINK
WHY IS IT SO? ROCK SAID I DO NOT EGZAGERATE
  OVER IT NOW
GETTING UP BUT I RUN NOTHING BUT A ROCK

TWIST

Suffice it to say that while this interpretation speaks volumes about the writer's sheer tenacity, not to mention songwriting abilities, it has little to do with the actual content of Korn's "Twist."

Like "Sean Olson," the song "Chi" was also named after a friend of the band, specifically the Deftones' bassist, Chi Cheng. While Jonathan has said that the song is "about a lot of alcohol and drug abuse," it was named "Chi" for the sole reason that Chi loved reggae and had taken it into his head that "Chi" was actually a reggae tune. Writing "Mr. Rogers," Jonathan took a trip down nostalgia's dark alley, back to his days as a naive schoolboy who'd followed the insidious advice of Mr. Rogers right into the loser's corner. He'd begun working on the song back in the fall of 1995, while the band was still on tour, and picked up the thread now that he was stuck in a Magic Hotel room.

Jonathan's obsession with Mr. Rogers, the man and the song, defied all reason. Observe: "Back in the day when I was a speed freak, um . . . even further back when I was a little kid watchin' Mr. Rogers, that shit was scary. He was a freaky old man . . . Land of Make-Believe and Mr. Fuckin' McFeely and shit . . . made me sick. So back when I was doing speed, like for five or six days I'd be trippin out and my brain would start to get freaky and get schizophrenic and stuff, and I'd tape it and watch it every day over and over . . . I don't know, I was sick in the head. As a kid he told me to be polite, and all it did was get me picked on. I fucking hate that man. Thanks for making me polite and trusting everyone, and easy to take advantage of. So I spent three months on that one song, just tweakin' on it, and it was totally just my Mr. Rogers obsession, about how evil I thought he was. Pretty much drug-induced."

The frontman has referred to his singing on Korn's first two albums as "straight fuckin' cathartic rage," and after considering the feelings that had incubated "Mr. Rogers," along with "K@#%!," "Good God," and "Kill You," it's fair to say that he was not one for hyperbole. On the latter ditty, he lashes out at the stepmother who'd force-fed him Tabasco sauce, and whom he'd dreamt of killing all those nights so many years ago. "K@#%!" was a scathing, invective-saturated indictment of all the women who'd hurt him in the past, and as such, he knew that it was bound to get him into hot water with NOW activists everywhere. Some months later, he'd have to do some fancy back-pedaling, explaining that "people are, like, saying I'm a woman-hater and shit, but I'm not. Sure, there are some women I hate, but there are also some men I hate. And that's what that song's about. I don't hate women. But this album just has many different sides to my lyrics."

To prove the veracity of his claims, Jonathan could always point to "Good God," the powder keg of a track dedicated to flaying a false friend of some eight years prior. In case you hadn't noticed, this is one vocalist who knows how to hold a grudge. According to the songwriter, the song is "about a guy I knew in school who I thought was my friend, but who fucked me. He came into my life with nothing, hung out at my house, lived off me, and made me do shit I didn't really wanna do. I was into New Romantic music and he was a Mod, and he'd tell me if I didn't dress like a Mod he wouldn't be my friend anymore. Whenever I had plans to go on a date with a chick he'd sabotage it, because he didn't have a date or nothing. He was a gutless fucking nothing. I haven't talked to him for years."

Subject matter for the rest of the tracks ran the gamut from schoolyard humor ("A.D.I.D.A.S.," as in *all day I dream about sex*") to songwriter's block ("Ass Itch" as in

"I hate writing shit, it is so stupid"). Taken as a whole, Jonathan's writing on the sophomore album did not reach the visceral level of intensity achieved on *Korn*. These songs were the product of a man who had the advantage of perspective, a man who'd already exhumed his vilest of demons and dealt with them accordingly. Obviously, the anguish was still there, but the writer's excessive ruminations upon his torment, as opposed to the situations which had ignited it, showed a marked desire to unearth and celebrate pain for its own sake.

Jonathan's bandmates, however, couldn't have been any more pleased with their frontman's efforts. On one prior occasion, Brian had been heard to joke that he hoped "that Jonathan doesn't get help; we're screwed if he gets cured." Since the singer's lyrics had all of that desperate aggression that had become Korn's trademark, there was no reason to doubt either the effect they'd have on the audience, or the authenticity of their impact upon Jonathan himself. To be fair, in the face of a time shortage and a highly satisfying way of life, Jonathan had done an admirable job excavating and transcribing the painful memories of years past.

Yet when he described the rationale behind the chosen album title, *Life Is Peachy*, Jonathan unwittingly revealed that, unlike on *Korn*—where he had written and sung purely for the sake of his own sanity—this album was structured primarily around the needs and demands of the band's newfound demographic: the troubled teen. "We all know that life isn't peachy," he said. "For a lot of people it's really tough. The funny part is that everyone thinks that just because we've sold a few records and spent a year on the road that our lives are totally peachy now. Well, it's not bad, but we're not really talkin' about ourselves in the title. This is a tough, harsh record about a tough, harsh world. It certainly ain't peachy out there."

By the end of May, Korn were ready to begin the *Life Is Peachy* recording sessions. Given their past antipathy for the Malibu sun, it's odd that they chose to return to Indigo Ranch Studios. Whether the decision was due to time constraints or to the group members' increasingly sunny dispositions is uncertain, but there's no denying that living and recording at Indigo Ranch allowed the group to get away from L.A.'s sundry distractions and immerse themselves in the business of making music. With only three months left to get the job done, the guys couldn't afford to take any chances.

The rushed pace didn't agree with the musicians, who would have liked to spend more time before bagging the takes. "For the new record we went in really fresh, and we wanted to get it done quickly to capture the energy," David dissembled for the press. "So it was probably about sixty percent knowing what I was going to play and forty percent just playing whatever came to mind at that moment. I laid down about three songs a day and finished all my tracks in five days. I don't think I did more than three takes on any of the songs I recorded. I was a little nervous doing it that way, because I didn't want to throw off some good fills and then be unhappy with them later on. But it ended up really good, and it has a kind of energy I probably wouldn't have gotten if I'd worked out everything beforehand."

The stickman has since admitted that capturing the energy was, in fact, the least of Korn's reasons for hastening the recording process. The pressure, he said, was actually rooted more in marketing concerns "than anything else, because November and December are pretty bad times to release albums. That's when labels are concentrating on their Christmas albums, and we didn't want to get overshadowed by all that. We figured if we put it out in October and started touring right away, we would pick up momentum as the tour went on."

High atop their Malibu mountain, the group was so completely removed from reality that they decided to make "K@#%!" their first single. Thinking that they'd be pulling a fast one on all the radio stations bent on censoring Jonathan's lyrics, the guys couldn't wait to hear the programmers' response to their latest opus. The song had the double advantage of eviscerating every one of Jonathan's ball-breaking ex-girlfriends, while at the same time providing kids with a fun, foul-language tune to launch into on schoolbus singalongs. "We were gonna [send it to radio] as a joke 'cause we knew they wouldn't play it, then follow up about a week later with the real thing," Munky explained.

However, Jonathan's intentions regarding the song appeared to be far more serious than the run-of-the-mill rock-star buffoonery. Feeling put-out and under duress, he viewed "K@#%!" as a testament to Korn's independent spirit. "I'm so tired of [the radio people] cutting my cuss words out. That's how I sing, and this is to make a stand. We're throwing a big wrench into the fucker," he asserted. "We've got this far without radio stations and MTV. We really don't give a fuck. Record companies just want to make a quick buck and then go, 'Next band, please.' If we let people get their meathooks into us, it'd spoil a good thing."

A few months later, the record company would indeed shoot down the band's request to play a joke on the radio stations. So Korn's latest and greatest strike against corporate America never happened. It was just as well, for according to Fieldy, it was not as if the band really "wanted it to happen." Playing with the outrageous notion had been just another source of amusement for a group of guys who were none too thrilled with their confinement to the Indigo Ranch compound. Certainly, there had been many more wild ideas where that one came from. If one discounted the loud ticking of the countdown to the October release date, the *Life Is Peachy* sessions would have been nearly indistinguishable from Korn's previous forays into the studio. As always, Ross was a constant fixture in the console room, working tirelessly to cheer on his world-weary and studio-wan charges.

Much like on the debut album, Jonathan felt the need for a producer more acutely than did his fellow bandmates. Truth be told, the singer actually required that everyone within shooting distance observe his moments in the vocal booth. As many as fifteen people could often be found crowding the studio while Jonathan cut his tracks. Although the rest of Korn laughed off this small compulsion on the part of their lead singer, saying that "he likes to show off," the guys knew Jonathan well enough to understand his deep-seated desire for affirmation and support. As much as he loved hearing positive reviews, often claiming that they made all the effort worthwhile, he hated the negative ones that much more.

In the end, the band wrapped up *Life Is Peachy* just in the nick of time. Of course, there would be misgivings down the line. Had it not been for the external prodding from the record company and management, the LP could, would, and should have been an improvement over *Korn*. As things stood, however, the guys had to summon all their strength to get behind the sophomore album that was to be their bid for longevity. They would succeed in these attempts—but not for long. Two years later, Jonathan would explain that "*Life Is Peachy* was the direction we wanted to go, but we were so rushed . . . We weren't that proud of *Peachy*. At first we were, but to live with it, no. We were just so rushed, it sucked."

Unwilling to let their new CD debut in discount dust-

bins all over America, Korn refrained from voicing such
sentiments until long after the album's release. The key
now was to begin building anticipation for the new record. With the press finally taking notice, the guys had to
become a group of quasi–spin doctors, and fast. When
asked, they'd invariably ascribe the short recording schedule to their own eagerness, never mentioning the merce-
nary nature of their true motivations. In describing the
forthcoming album, they'd use only the most glowing
terms, going so far as to imply that their debut disc would
actually suffer in comparison to this latest oeuvre. To say
that they were deliberately misleading the public, however, would be to do the band a grave injustice. At least
for the time being, Korn believed every word of their own
hype.

In 1996, Korn not only found the time to record an album, but to play live shows numbering in the triple digits
as well. To accomplish the feat, the band had had to resume their death-defying tour schedule as soon as the *Life
Is Peachy* recording sessions wound down. One of their
first shows was headlining the second stage at the U.K.'s
Donington '96 Festival on August 17. With countless
thousands expected to arrive, Donington was to be another baptism-by-fire for the band that had spent all summer cooped up in a recording studio.

   According to Jonathan, the band was "shocked, honored
and freaked out by the thought of playing the festival." The
mother of all heavy-metal spectaculars, Donington could
intimidate simply by virtue of its sheer magnitude. But
given the fact that readers of *Kerrang!* magazine had voted
for Korn to headline the *Kerrang!* stage, the guys were
thrilled to show their faces. They'd be coming on after
bands such as Everclear and Type O Negative, and playing
just a stone's throw away from the main stage, which fea-

tured old friends Ozzy Osbourne and KISS as co-headliners. After the show, Korn were slated to play yet another festival, and then another, and then another after that, until the summer season wound to a close and the band returned to tour the States. But as Jonathan explained, "[Donington] is the biggest festival of its type in the world."

Even this knowledge couldn't prepare the group for the unfathomable mass of humanity that had gathered for the event. The sight of the sun shining down on all those bare torsos, tattoos, and piercings made every one of Korn's previous shows look infinitesimal by comparison. The band took the stage to find themselves confronted by a kaleidoscopic blanket of heads, shoulders, and arms that reached as far as the eye could see. In a post-performance interview with MTV Europe, Jonathan would express his awe: "I can't say nothing. I have no words explaining what I just saw there. I had no clue that it would be that intense . . . It was incredible. We had no clue. I just went up there and shocked the shit out of me, basically."

As soon as they began to play, it became clear that Korn had forgotten none of the tricks they'd picked up during their two years on the road. They played all the standards, like "Divine," "Shoots and Ladders," and "Faget," and further highlighted Jonathan's bagpipe-blowing prowess by including the War cover "Lowrider," from *Life Is Peachy*. A wild pit erupted just a few minutes into their set, and didn't break up until well after Korn had descended the stage, leaving all shouts for an encore unanswered.

After bounding off the scaffold, it was all the quintet could do to keep their wits about them for the press. They'd hardly slept the night before, and this latest exertion had hastened the onset of delirium. "I'm going to go to sleep," a spent Munky told the cameras, knowing full well that a rising rock star's work is never done, and that the next day would be just another trip through the portals of Bedlam.

One can just picture the reaction of *Rolling Stone* and *Entertainment Weekly* readers in the last weeks of October 1996, when these magazines made the latest *Billboard* charts available to music-industry outsiders nationwide.

"What the hell is Korn?"

"*Life Is Peachy*? Never heard of it."

"Can this be right?"

The album was ranked number three, and to be fair, laypeople weren't the only ones disoriented by the breaking news. The band members themselves—not to mention their jubilant families, managers, and record-label personnel—could hardly believe the printed and irrefutable proof of their monstrous popularity.

Prior to the October 15, 1996, release, Immortal Records had already sent out advance copies of the album to the media. Each promotional unit contained a missive informing the beneficiary that they would either grow heady with joy at the mere thought of hearing the latest from Korn, or take the offending tape and, with all due haste, aim it straight for the trash can. In other words, you'd either love 'em or leave 'em—with this band, there was no in between.

From this buildup, it is easy to grasp why Fieldy was overcome with tears of joy at the sight of his band's name nestled in the top three of the *Billboard* 200. Even his wildest expectations fell short of the reality. "When they told us *Life Is Peachy* debuted at number three on the charts," he later confessed. "I cry over the stupidest shit."

Stupid or not, the favorable ranking lifted Korn out of the underground once and for all. Nay, *almost* once and for all. MTV and radio had yet to show the biggest name in New Metal anything in the way of love. Having scrapped their plans to shock the bejezus out of radio programmers with "K@#%!," the band decided that the accessible "A.D.I.D.A.S." would be the track to bear the distinguished title of lead single.

The guys were once again called upon to make a video. While their former attempts on this front had amounted to little more than an exercise in futility, the tastemakers were finally listening. This time, the label assured them, Korn's videos would get airplay. Just as the group was plotting out the concept, they got a call from a well-known music-video director who'd been reading up on the band. His idea would soon be turned into Korn's "A.D.I.D.A.S." video, the one that most of the band's current fans fondly recall as their first taste of Korn.

The gist of it was to follow the guys as they drive in their car, die in a high-speed collision, and are taken to the morgue in body bags and placed on mortuary slabs. The shoot lasted a full day, and left the group with a better sense of their own limitations. "It was fun," recounted Fieldy. "The only thing that I didn't like too much was being zipped up in that body bag—and I didn't like putting the contacts in my eyes. I guess the worst part of the video was towards the end of the video when we were laying on those tables—we had to lay on those tables for about five hours. It fucking sucked, man! I don't really think I would ever have the patience to act."

No sooner had the single and its accompanying video hit radio stations and the MTV offices, than "A.D.I.D.A.S." was in frequent rotation, and teens nationwide were hailing the band as the long-awaited antidote to the Hanson epidemic. Print media was also picking up and running with the Korn banner. A reviewer from the *Chicago Tribune* had this to say: "If Korn wasn't so sarcastic about it, they could have titled their second album *Life Is Lunacy*. Here we have an assembly of twisted souls—perverts, psychopaths, and paranoiacs—dramatized by the creepy multipersonality soliloquies of singer Jonathan Davis. What emerges is an overload of troubled emotion: thrashy hiphop, the vocal spasms of Davis and guitarist Head, and a sound that is both grooved and jagged." A critic from *Scream* magazine was no less impressed, bestowing the album with five out of a possible six points, and calling it "much more aggressive, extreme and industrial. This is a right in your face album. Total madness."

In a year's time, after people had had sufficient time to digest the warped modulations of *Life Is Peachy*, more accolades would be forthcoming. While many of those who'd been following Korn's every step since the release of their debut record weren't as enthusiastic as their newly initiated brethren, the general consensus seemed to be that *Life Is Peachy* did not disappoint. Given the rushed recording process, that was an accomplishment all in itself.

And yet most of the mainstream publications persisted in dismissing the band as irrelevant studio hacks. Behold the write-up of *Entertainment Weekly*'s David Grad:

Korn's sophomore release may be of interest to mental-health professionals, but there is no reason for even the most twisted thrash-metal fans to expose themselves to this fifty-minute self-indulgent primal scream. Profanity-driven rants like the aptly titled "K@#%!" or "Kill You" undermine the band's compelling fusion of heavy riffs and tight hip-hop beats, leaving the impression that frontman Jonathan Davis is turning his well-publicized childhood traumas into a cheap marketing device. C−.

This latter bit of smug Korn-bashing sent Jonathan straight into paroxysms of rage. According to the pissed-off vocalist, the critic had been way out of line, and Jonathan was not above verbal retaliation. "Who's this fucking bastard to say that?" he fired back. "These are my feelings you're talking about and I'm not putting my feelings out to make money at all. I'm putting my feelings out for myself and other people; if I get money, that just comes with it, but I'm not one to be money-hungry. Fuck them, fuck those scared little bastards."

And with that, the band set off to capitalize on their hard-won notoriety. Often selling out shows in a matter of minutes, they returned to America's midsized venues, this time as triumphant headliners. Supported by Limp Bizkit, and greeted by auditoriums of "Korn kids," the band without a genre to call their own had finally succeeded in hammering out a niche. A little bit hip-hop, a little bit heavy-metal, the quintet defied categorization, and at long last, their fans did, too.

After bringing their brand of noise into a few dozen U.S. hamlets, opening several Metallica concerts, and taking some much needed time off to bond with their live-in girlfriends over the holidays, Korn braced themselves for the European leg of their tour. Considering the fact that their last Euro-trek was an experience best left to memory block, the guys were decidedly underwhelmed by the repeat engagement. But all that would change once the band encountered the Korn-starved European masses on January 21, 1997.

Kicking off in Hamburg, Germany, the guys would pass through no less than eight cities in the U.K., four in Germany, four in France, two in Spain, and one each in Austria, Sweden, Italy, Denmark, Norway, and the Netherlands, before winding down in London on February 24.

This last was a rain-check performance necessitated by the tour-induced illness that had kept Jonathan from taking the stage on February 1.

One look at Korn's itinerary says it all. Twenty-six shows in thirty-four days. Pity the poor bands—Incubus and the Urge—that had agreed to open for our road-faring heroes. Not that the tour was any easier on the members of Korn. Unwilling to let their relationships buckle under the pressure of the road, the guys would call their girlfriends every night from their hotel rooms. David, who was expecting a baby, was especially vigilant—not to mention distraught. "It wasn't so bad before, when I didn't really have a home that was my home, with all my belongings in, and when I didn't have a girl waiting for me, when I had nobody I cared about," he related. "I wasn't missing anybody. I always miss my family, but I'm used to being away from them. So it wasn't that big a deal. I'd be out on tour and I'd look forward to going home just to get off the road and be able to drive around in my car and hang out with my friends. I'd miss that. But it's different now that I have somebody that I love and I'm starting a family with. It's a whole different story. That's a different kind of missing."

Whereas Jonathan and Fieldy shared their drummer's remorse and longing, Brian managed to sidestep cruel destiny by bringing his girlfriend, Rebekkah Ricketts, on board for what had to be the most hectic vacation of her young life. "It's hard, you know, being gone on tour all the time and having a relationship," Brian affirmed. "She has a hard time sometimes. This year I've seen her a lot. She came out to Europe for ten days, so that's good. We go with it. It just gets hard sometimes."

Spending two months out of the year with one's nearest and dearest can drive anyone to distraction. Even Jonathan, who could usually rely on a series of post-show endorphin highs to carry him through Korn's tours, took to questioning his chosen way of life. "I miss Nathan and Renée a lot," he reported, "but I wouldn't do that to them—dragging them all over the world with me would be cruel. Touring is really crazy!!! It's such a weird feeling, last time I saw him he was a toddler and now he is already walking! I love music and I feel I have something to say but sometimes I wonder if it is worth it."

And yet, if concert reviews are any indication, customer satisfaction more than made up for Korn's ups and downs on the road to world domination. With MTV Europe spinning "A.D.I.D.A.S." as if it were the only Korn single to date, and the European press agog over the band's every vitriolic vocal and ear-rending run, the quintet drew mammoth crowds, selling out ballroom after dance hall. At every venue, lines of Adidas-clad, Korn T-shirt–sporting fans stretched from the doors, down the street, and around the block. In concert, the group could do no wrong. Minutes into their fifteen-song sets, the slam-dancing and stage-diving would commence to surpass the bounds of mere jostling until finally reaching a desperate, "run for your life, it's going to blow" frenzy. At tour's end, *Kerrang!* expressed the sentiments of everyone who'd come, seen, and been subjugated by, the brutal force of Korn: "If you missed this tour, it was probably the biggest mistake of your year."

The Korn-fed crowds urged the band to press on, to forget about their life's loves and just rock out, if only for a few months more. However, these rallying cries were not the band's sole source of inspiration. Thoughts of the months ahead also helped to sustain the guys through their marathon tour schedule.

Rumors of the band's summer plans had begun to circulate before Korn had even left the States. Word had it that Korn would get the nod to headline the biggest name in U.S. rock festivals—none other than Perry Farrell's brainchild, Lollapalooza. While the final verdict had yet to be announced, the guys had it on good authority that the deal was as good as done. But summer was still a full season in the coming, and Korn had a more immediate boon brightening their horizon. In January 1997, the music industry had effectively turned the tables on the ensemble, shocking them straight out of their "we're still an underground band" reverie. Lo and behold, Korn was now a Grammy-nominated outfit.

The National Academy of Recording Arts and Sciences (NARAS) had seen fit to endow "Shoots and Ladders" with a nomination for Best Metal Performance. Korn would be going head-to-head with such long-lived artists as Rob Zombie and Alice Cooper, Pantera, White Zombie, and Rage Against the Machine. Despite the band's anti-establishment stance, the token of recognition made even this hardcore outfit feel all warm and fuzzy inside. For Jonathan, the nomination was proof positive of his success, a symbol that even his careworn parents could finally understand. "The big thing was when we got the Grammy nomination," he recollected, "then [my parents] were like, ['Okay, you've made it']. I want that fuckin' Grammy. I used to be a little kid who'd watch that show every year and fantasize about being up on the stage and all that shit. It's my childhood dream: I want a Grammy."

Judging by Jonathan's words, Korn was not a band to thumb their noses at NARAS in misguided protest. The guys planned to attend the 39th Annual Grammy Awards ceremony, tuxedo and all. The event, scheduled to be held on February 27, would mark their victorious return to the U.S.—win or lose.

8
the agony and the ekstasy

February of 1997 would not, as it turned out, transform Korn into a group of Grammy Award winners. Instead, the gold-plated gramophone would go to Rage Against the Machine for "Tire Me." Which was fine, for while Korn certainly wanted that trophy, they definitely didn't need it to further their upwardly mobile career. A week after the ceremony, the band was out doing what they've always done best—inciting riots in auditorium pits across the nation.

Having put the European push to bed only ten days ago, the guys had had scarcely enough time to see their friends and families, check out the new EP of "A.D.I.D.A.S." remixes as well as the final cut of their *Who Then Now?* home video, and congratulate Fieldy on his girlfriend Shela's pregnancy, before returning to work. On March 6, 1997, the band was already in Mesa, Arizona, playing to a packed Mesa Amphitheater. From there, it was on to Denver, Kansas City, New Orleans, Pensacola, Tampa, Orlando, Athens, Louisville, Dayton, Milwaukee, St. Paul, Chicago, Akron, Toronto, and a final March 27 performance in Lewiston, Maine. All told, the band saw sixteen cities—or more specifically, sixteen hotel rooms and venues—in three weeks.

While this was by no means a new record for the hardest-working outfit in rock, they still planned to take a much-deserved breather before heading out with Lollapalooza. An extended vacation would have been the ideal reward for the band that had shifted some two million units. After learning that their debut album and *Life Is Peachy* had gone platinum and gold respectively, not even the loss of a Grammy could have put a damper on their soaring spirits. Their once-empty mantels now boasted two gleaming plaques, and while each still reserved space for the music industry's most coveted statuette, just gazing at the material evidence of their public's affection brought the hardened men of Korn to the point of contented sighing.

In fact, Jonathan might well have spent all spring doing just that, if the record company had not alerted his band to the latest in late-breaking news: *Life Is Peachy* had gone gold in Australia. Touring arrangements would have to be made forthwith. "We didn't even know how it happened," recalled Fieldy. "When our record company said, 'You have a gold record in Australia'—we're like, 'How?' We don't even know, then they tell us about how it is doin' on the charts and we're like, 'Well, that's cool—I guess we gotta go there now.' "

April, of course, was out of the question. David Silveria's plans had blocked off the entire month. He and Shannon Bellino, his five-months-pregnant girlfriend, were getting married. To commemorate the union and reaffirm his commitment, David had *Shannon* tattooed on his back. But the honeymoon was over before the ink on his backside had even had a chance to set. Korn rounded up their road crew and headed for the Land Down Under.

The trip was scheduled to last ten days, but the maddening flight schedule made it feel more like twenty. Korn had grown used to tooling about in the privacy of their tour bus, where they had beds, a TV, a VCR, an expansive video collection, and a well-stocked refrigerator-freezer. Jetting about, on the other hand, required that the band members roll out of bed at ungodly hours, repair for the airport, and endure the inevitably interminable wait. At length, the fifteen-hour plane ride that finally transported the guys back to LAX brought a most appropriate end to Korn's Australian fly-about.

With Lollapalooza '97 still about a month away, the band could have whiled away the hours by resting upon their hard-won laurels, or, at the very least, by spending some rare moments with the mothers of their children and children-to-be. Like Shannon Silveria, Fieldy's girlfriend Shela Avina was also in her second trimester. Meanwhile, Jonathan's son was now a walking and baby-talking one-and-a-half-year-old. The singer's absence made little Nathan's aging process seem just like so much time-lapse photography, and Jonathan didn't like it at all.

"I am going down the same road my dad did," he revealed. "It's killing me, because I'm doing what my dad did to me, in that I'm always on the road, but I tell myself that I'm making his life better in the future. He'll be pissed off with me, probably get in a band and write songs about me, and that would make me the happiest man in the world."

As if to secure this future happiness for Jonathan, Korn spent the month prior to Lollapalooza missing in action. In Europe, the music festival season was again in full swing, and the band had gone off in search of still more fans. On June 3, the band brought a long-in-the-planning scheme to fruition by broadcasting their London concert at the Brixton Academy live over the Internet at www.korn.com. Korn did not hide their motivations—not only did they want to satisfy the needs of their existent fan base, but they wanted to bring their music to as many of the Korn-deprived multitudes as possible. Many was the time that their late-night cyberchats with curious fans deprived the guys of that rarest of luxuries: sleep.

When the June launch of Lollapalooza rolled around, a second wind made the group's listlessness a thing of the past. This was their dream, and they were ready to seize upon it like birds of prey on carrion. They'd played so many outdoor gigs, provoked so much mayhem, and played their no-longer-new songs so damn often, that they could have done Lollapalooza with both hands tied behind their tattooed backs.

But there would be no going through the motions on this summer tour. One cannot overestimate the special importance that Lollapalooza had for the quintet. Ever since its storied 1991 inception, the tour had held a large place in Korn's collective heart. As David remarked, "It's the coolest tour for a summer festival I've ever seen. It always has been."

The array of legendary names that had played the Lolla' stages, and the endless roster of new artists that had broken out of obscurity during those summers, combined to lend the festival a magical quality that has stayed with it through good times and bad. And there had been some bad times. By many accounts, the summer of 1996 had marked one such low point in Lolla' lore. When grand marquee players such as Metallica and Soundgarden had deigned to perform, founder Perry Farrell walked off in disgust over what he saw as the bastardization of his festival's good name. But with Korn, Tool, Snoop Doggy Dogg, Tricky, Orbital, Orb, and Prodigy all slated to headline Lollapalooza '97, Farrell had come out of his self-imposed exile for the June 26 opening in West Palm Beach, Florida.

Parsing over the list of artists, Jonathan could understand the impresario's change of heart. "Last year . . . wasn't like a real Lollapalooza vibe," he explained, "because it seems to me that Lollapalooza's been about cutting-edge bands, ones on the underground, and that's what I think he based that whole thing on and last year really just wasn't all about that. And this year, now that he's back on, you can tell, there's so many different, diverse music groups here."

Sure enough, the tour featured acts of all shapes and sizes; music from every corner of the sonic spectrum was represented. Techno, alt-rock, rap metal, gangsta rap, heavy metal, reggae . . . there was something for everyone, just like its creator had intended. However, the biggest surprise to emerge out of all this variety was the utter preponderance of Korn fans who'd flocked to watch the defiant ones stomp the main stage. Kornmania was the talk of the festival, as many bands either named the band among their Lolla '97 favorites, or threw barbs at the just-arrived rockers and their endless supply of Korn logo–flaunting fans. As always, there was no middle ground.

As throngs of spectators went stark raving mad during Korn's performance, the band asserted their dominance and continued to eclipse the myriad of illustrious names on Lolla's lineup for the duration of their tenure. Undeterred by the other artists on the Lollapalooza bill, Korn fans were coming out of the woodwork to buy tickets and voice their support. With Tool enjoying a similar measure of success, it seemed as though metal was the hands-down favorite of all the festival's disparate genres.

Bussing it by night, carousing and performing by day, and chumming it up with the likes of Snoop Doggy Dogg by dusk, Jonathan could describe the vibe only as "one big party." Like the rest of the participants, Korn had come to see and be seen. They'd wanted to meet the bands whose music they loved, and to hear the sounds of bands whose music they'd only heard of. They were especially eager to meet Prodigy, who were scheduled to join the tour toward the end of July. Sadly, force majeur intervened just in time to trump Korn's plans for an introduction and a possible collaboration.

For nearly three weeks, the tour had gone like clockwork. MTV had actually begun to woo Korn, giving them a video camera to shoot their own mini-rockumentary and referring to them (on the air!) as "one of our favorite new bands." The fans were also in top form. From fashioning the provided seating into crowd-surfing boards, to kicking up clouds of dust in the pits, audiences were uninhibited in displaying their unbridled love for Korn. At one stop, the guys were walking around the festival grounds, taking in the scenery, when a group of about fifteen concertgoers approached them. The laid-back musicians went with the flow, talking to the fans mano a mano, and shaking their hands. When their goings-on caught the attention of a nearby crowd, Korn suddenly found themselves besieged by hundreds of clamoring kids, and fearing for their lives. Peace was restored only when security arrived to throw the rockers a lifeline. In retrospect, David had to admit that "that was a pretty good feeling, just to see these crazy kids think that our dumb asses were cool enough to do that to." The group could have easily ridden this wave of adulation all the way to the final tour date. Munky, however, could not carry on for so much as another day.

The guitarist's illness began to make itself felt only two weeks into the tour. While Munky had been having as much fun as anybody, drinking, hanging out, and joking with MTV's Serena Altschul, his spirits dipped after the festival had wrapped up its July 15 engagement at Michigan's Pine Knob Music Theater. On the way to the next

Lolla stop, the axman began suffering from migraines and nausea. His condition took a sharp turn for the worse after Korn played their July 18 set in Ohio. To this day, Munky recalls the ensuing events as the nadir of his artistic career.

"It was pretty confusing when I first got sick because I really didn't know what was happening to me, I wasn't sure what I had," he later explained. "I wanted to die. Literally. I was so sick. I had migraine headaches and I was vomiting. I was completely miserable. I was stressed out. I didn't know what was going on with me. I also didn't want to leave the tour because I knew it was one of the band's longtime dreams to be on the Lollapalooza tour."

When Munky was taken to the hospital, he was at the end of his rope, physically and mentally. "The only thing I was thinking about . . . was when was I going to get better so I could get back out on tour," he said. "I was just in pain—physical pain. And it was so horrible because it was causing me mental pain because I wasn't sure what I had."

After doctors had a chance to examine the ailing musician, they came back with a frightening diagnosis: viral meningitis. Fortunately, the problem had been caught in time and, with a little hospitalization, Munky would be just fine. As far as Korn were concerned, they had no choice but to bow out of the tour. "I really didn't care about quitting Lollapalooza," Brian said. "It was a really fun tour and I cared about that, but I wasn't thinking, 'Oh man, we had to cancel.' I just wanted Munky to get better because the more we heard about what he had, the more serious it sounded."

Friends first, business partners and bandmates second, the group would not so much as think of continuing without their right-hand guitarist. While the tour promoters urged them to press on, the guys maintained that "there is no suitable replacement for Munky during his recuperation." They were staying put. "I didn't even think twice about it," Brian said. "I just wanted him to get better." Within a week of the incident, Team Korn had issued a written statement. In it, Jonathan said: "We love our fans. This is the last thing we want to do, but it's the only decision to make at this time. It just doesn't feel right without Munky."

Although quitting Lollapalooza was a blow for the band that had built the tour's importance up to mythic proportions, it was one from which they would recover just as surely as Munky would live to play guitar again. Testifying to the band's widespread and firmly entrenched appeal was the *Kerrang!* Awards ceremony of August 1997. Nominated for several of the magazine's Readers' Choice awards, Korn had been cordially invited to put in an appearance. With Munky out of commission, David unable to leave his wife's ample, nine-months-pregnant side, and Head otherwise engaged in spending rare quality time with his neglected girlfriend, the attendance duties fell to Jonathan and Fieldy.

The day of the awards ceremony saw the lethargic pair trudging their way to LAX and embarking upon the morning flight to London. Looking all the worse for wear, the guys showed up at the Royal Lancaster Hotel early to partake of libations prior to the ceremony. When the proceedings got under way, the guys were dismayed to hear Korn being passed over for one award after the next. After losing out on three awards in a row, Fieldy and Jonathan looked at each other in utter disbelief. They'd come a long way for cocktails.

Coincidentally, the last award of the evening was also the band's last opportunity to score. Nervous apprehension prevailed as the presenter began: "The nominees for

Best Album are . . . Foo Fighters for *The Colour and the Shape*; Machine Head for *The More Things Change* . . . ; Jon Bon Jovi for *Destination Anywhere*; Korn for *Life Is Peachy*; and Marilyn Manson for *Antichrist Superstar*."

The tension was so pronounced, Jonathan and Fieldy could have sworn they heard a drum roll. If Korn didn't win now, they expected to feel nothing short of total and complete mortification.

"And the winner for Best Album is . . . Korn, for *Life Is Peachy*."

No sooner had their name been announced, than Jonathan and Fieldy were on their feet, bounding for the podium.

"It's our very first award ever," Jonathan said, trying to explain away his distinctly angst-free exuberance, "and we really are honored."

"And because it's our first award, we'll remember it forever," Fieldy confirmed. "I just thank the readers. We love you!"

With the awards at a happy end, the friends set off for the afterparties. They would need to remain in London for another two days just to give interviews. While the Q&A sessions were not in themselves remarkable, Jonathan would come home from the trip full of lasting memories. Aside from winning his first award, he also managed to run into his first rock idol, Duran Duran frontman Simon Le Bon. While the meeting left Jonathan feeling that Le Bon's best days were indeed behind him, his initial response was one of starstruck stupefaction. "I got to meet Simon Le Bon last night," he revealed to one interviewer, "and I thought I was gonna faint! You just have teen idols that you look up to."

The fact that Jonathan and his four bandmates still kept their childhood heroes up on their rightful pedestals, shed light on Korn's behavior toward their own fans. On many prior occasions, they had affirmed that, although they were a full ten years older than their average fan, they could relate to their teenaged listeners as readily as if they, too, were still in high school. The twenty-somethings remembered exactly what it had felt like to admire, emulate, and cherish a rock band. Thus it was the thought of their fans' disappointment, more than any fear for their own fiscal welfare, that caused the band such anguish over the aborted Lollapalooza mission, and such consternation over the outcome of their next studio venture.

After passing ten long days in his hospital room, Munky was discharged. The prognosis was promising: the guitarist would be as good as new—that is, provided he stuck to the recovery regimen. A few weeks of bed rest were mandatory.

Since Korn had long planned to follow up the festival with three weeks of relaxation, and then an intensive round of songwriting, Munky's illness served only to accelerate their return to the rehearsal studio. The third album had been the subject of much anxiety-inducing discussion within the Korn camp. Despite the positive reviews and fan support for their sophomore CD, no one was happy with the way *Life Is Peachy* had turned out. Unwilling to be rushed through yet another recording process, the band wanted to begin studio work as soon as possible and have their new album out in the first quarter of 1998.

Of course, the studio would have to wait for Munky's full recovery. The guitar parts, according to Head, just wouldn't have been the same without him. "I think the combination of my guitar with Munky's makes our sound more interesting and doubly creative," he expressed. "He thinks of stuff I wouldn't think of, and I think of stuff that he wouldn't think of. It's like we're one person. We're one guitar player thinking."

The axman's poor health, however, was by no means the only impediment barring the band's road to the studio. No sooner had Munky left the hospital than another member of Korn's extended family was admitted. This time, however, the occasion was a happy one. David and Shannon were having a baby. On August 22, 1997, David Silveria, Jr., came bursting into the world. With celebratory cigars the order of the day, crafting songs was temporarily relegated to the farthest reaches of the backburner.

we're not going to settle

The autumnal season has traditionally been associated with death and decay, but Korn have never been the type of band to abide by the laws of convention. Fall 1998 would be the group's most fecund season to date, giving rise to some of their greatest achievements and imbuing their career with a longevity that would have naysayers eating their words. The September 30 birth of Fieldy's daughter, Sarina Rae, only hinted at the renaissance that was still to come. Certainly, even the members of Korn were not aware that the work which began that autumn would become the lifeblood of the heavy rock revival.

The two priorities uppermost on the bandmates' minds were their new album and their new record label. With the arrival of David's and Fieldy's babies, the majority of the band had crossed the final threshold into the worry-packed world of adulthood. As baby-toting members of the grown-up circle, they were no longer content to drift aimlessly from concert to studio and back. This was their cue to pick up the reins and steer their career into a future of their own making, and they were only too ready to accept the responsibility.

For some time now, the guys had been toying with the notion of starting up a record label. Signing bands that they liked, guiding them to greatness and making a little pocket money in the process was the type of gig that could keep them in the black for the rest of their days. And with children to think about, David, Jonathan, and Fieldy could no longer afford to let everything ride on the performance of their latest CD. Despite the many Korn loyalists who would undoubtedly stand in line for a concert ticket or a newly released album, the band was plagued by nagging fears. As Jonathan explained, "You've just got to think—I mean, this is a crucial fucking album in our career. And we've pretty much fucked our lives away doing this. If this doesn't come off, what am I gonna do with my life? . . . I was like, 'What am I gonna do? I've got a kid.' "

Motivated by the welfare of their beloved offspring, and bolstered by the wonders their support had done for Limp Bizkit's booming business, Korn were determined to hedge their bets by branching out into the executive suites. When probed about the inspiration for the new label, Jonathan replied without a moment's hesitation: "Finding [Limp Bizkit], getting them phat, taking them on the road with us for as long as we did," he explained. "And we were like, 'Fuck, we should have signed them to our own label.' "

Sensing that they were on to something, the group took their ideas and adjourned to Epic Records' headquarters. Since the record-company behemoth distributed the CDs for Korn's label, Immortal, common courtesy dictated that Epic get first right of refusal. Taking full advantage of this right, the label refused "to have any part of it," recalled Jonathan, "so we went to Warner Bros. and they were really down."

By November 1997, just three short years after releasing their very first album, all the pieces were in place and Elementree Records was officially Korn's to do with as they pleased. "It's our label," confirmed Jonathan, "but it's just distributed through [Reprise/Warner Bros.]"

Sure enough, the band had some definite ideas about what it was they wanted to do. "I think we'd all like to sign some bands that everybody's scared to sign," said Fieldy. "And, of course, to make them as big as Korn, if not bigger. I think where we're at in '98, the whole decade is really hurting for some good music."

What's more, the group was just as certain as to what they were *not* going to do. "[Elementree's] not going to be like a Nothing Records, where everything sounds like Trent Reznor," Jonathan promised. "Not everything is going to sound like Korn, but it has to be bad-ass. We're not going to settle."

That very month, Elementree Records signed their first band. Based upon a demo and Jonathan's passing acquaintance with Orgy guitarist Ryan Shuck, Korn gave the electronic glam-punk ensemble the green light. The record contract made for strange bedfellows, given the litigious nature of Korn's past relationship with Shuck. As the careful reader will recall, five years before Orgy was signed to Elementree, Jonathan and the guitar player were both members of SexArt. After the singer departed and SexArt disbanded, Shuck had noticed that Korn's debut album contained "Blind," one of SexArt's creations. Shuck promptly sued for credit. The lawsuit was settled out of court with the Orgy guitarist getting a share of the royalties and his name listed as co-writer.

By the time Korn got wind of Orgy, the hatchet had long since been buried. Shuck was contrite, saying "It's not cool to sue your friends," and Jonathan was head-over-Adidas for the demo, saying, "Orgy is just so dope." So not only would Elementree finance the band's first album, but Korn would also allow the new recruits to play as supporting act on their concert tour. A bold move, given that Orgy had only been in existence for six months, and Korn had yet to hear them in live performance. According to Orgy lead singer Jay Gordon, "The best thing, the very best thing about it all, is that we have a great label; it's fantastic to be a part of a label that's run by real people, guys like us, and not some guys in suits."

Korn's rock-star status would indeed work to their advantage in the realm of business. After commissioning Orgy, Jonathan lent his clout to their work-in-progress, *Candyass*, by singing on the album track "Revival." Fieldy would soon do likewise for the next act to sign with Elementree—Videodrone.

With their manager Jeff Kwatinetz helping them run Elementree, Korn were able to concurrently launch Orgy and begin pre-production on their own album. No longer capable of taking in the sounds of *Life Is Peachy* without cringing, the guys' main consideration for their third record was that it not be a rush job. For while the "get it done, get it done" mentality had netted them all the financial rewards of a hit, their new status was bereft of anything resembling pride of authorship. "We rushed *Peachy* a lot, which was our decision," Fieldy admitted. "Everybody, managers, we wanted to get back on tour, but after listening to *Peachy* we realized that rushing wasn't worth it."

Not about to make the same mistake again, the group had resolved early on that their next album wouldn't go out until they were good and ready. "We came off the road," recalled Jonathan, "and said, 'We're not going to settle this time, fuck that, we're just gonna write.'"

Indeed, this time things would be substantially different. In light of the many Korn knockoffs that had emerged since the band's meteoric rise to the top of the New Metal totem pole, the group decided to give their fabled Korn sound a much-needed overhaul. With everyone from Sepultura to Vanilla Ice calling upon Ross Robinson and cribbing Korn's signature chops, Jonathan reasoned that "everything was starting to sound the same and we needed to change it."

However, Korn's hiring of a new producer was as much a result of their new and vastly improved budget as it was of their wish to revamp their sound. *Life Is Peachy* had been made on a $150,000 shoestring. That factor had dictated their choice of both producers and studios. With $500,000 allocated to the completion of their latest CD, Malibu's 1902 Indigo Ranch studio gave way to North Hollywood's state-of-the-art NRG Recording, and Ross was traded for Steve Thompson of Guns 'N' Roses, Rollins Band, Butthole Surfers, and Blues Traveler acclaim. Fieldy's attitude was: "If you have money, then you can make things happen. Of course, it's gonna sound better."

Jonathan's approach was also a great departure from the past two albums. Whether it was the critical reviews or his own personal development that had colored his vision, his days of dredging up the traumas of childhood were over. Not only had he covered just about every issue that had plagued his coming-of-age, but he'd raved about them in concert night after night for three years running. It was time to add something of the latter-day Jonathan Davis to the mix. "I just talked about pretty much all I could say about my childhood and that kind of shit," he said. "I can't keep doing that—it's going to get stupid. I've got to keep doing new things."

The new album was to be the culmination of Korn's life's work. Everything the band had been, done, and seen would be embedded within its grooves. Four years in the business had altered their perspective, and to retain their integrity, the CD would have to reflect these changes. No longer satisfied with commercial success alone, the band aimed to prove themselves on the artistic front. "I knew we had it in us that we could do something great," expressed Jonathan, "fully integrate both albums and put out an album that we could really be proud of."

This was as ambitious an undertaking as the group had ever attempted. Trying to match their previous sales and not stray too far from their trademark groove while retaining their relevance in an environment teeming with copy-cats, brought the weight of the world to bear down upon the musicians' fatigued shoulders. Anticipating their third album had gotten the whole band into a mad tizzy. No one in the quintet had ever been this worried before. "The third album is really crucial," said Jonathan, by way of explanation. "We're over the sophomore jinx. But I think that the third album is more important than the second one. If it's good, you're set for the next ten years."

When *Life Is Peachy* was certified platinum in December 1997, the seemingly happy occasion served only to fuel the anxiety that already had the funk-thrash hucksters in a stranglehold. With so much hinging on the success of this album, there was no room for error. But neither could the band afford to play it safe. Remaining a viable and relevant heavy-rock outfit required that they forget their overriding stress, and focus on experimentation. To break out of the *Life Is Peachy* holding pattern, the guys had to go where no band had gone before. Such were the feelings that inspired the name of their third album—*Follow the Leader*.

The absence of Ross Robinson necessitated that the band members step up their participation in the production capacity. Although all had previously downplayed Ross's role, they had admitted to his key role in the rehearsal studio. When it came to identifying the valuable riffs and jump-starting the songs, Ross had been the man. Now that job fell to their new producer Steve Thompson. Not being as familiar with the band's machinations as his predecessor, Thompson, for all his acumen, could only do so much. Korn had to pick up the slack.

Fortunately, the band's hard-earned self-confidence strengthened their position in the studio to the point where they realized that they'd been producing their own sound all along. "Before, we never got to put our names on any of our albums which we did produce. We just gave it all to Ross," Jonathan said. "He was the cheerleader pretty much," Fieldy added, "and we were producing our shit." And so it was decided that on *Follow the Leader* Korn would share in the production credits.

In the first weeks of what would ultimately turn into a five-month pre-production process, the group tried a lot of different tacks to get their creative juices coursing. The standard procedures would have to be subverted in the name of musical progress. Whereas the guys used to work by laying down the instrumentals first and lyrics second, the possibility of discovering a new sound led them to reverse this order. "On this album, we were getting Jon to try writing lyrics without having a melody first," affirmed Fieldy. "We were just playing along with his words and let a melody come out as the words were flowing. So we did a little bit of different stuff on this album. We actually wrote a couple of music parts around a melody that he already had."

But as Fieldy said, these parts were few. After realizing that their new technique boasted no improvement over the old, the guys decided to get back to the drums, bass, guitars, vocals writing sequence that had served them so well on albums past. According to the bass guitarist, "That's how we write. Pretty much every song in that order. It's a process that works for us."

Of course, Korn's songwriting has never been an exact

science, and not all songs were constructed in such an orderly manner. "Got the Life" got its start with David's BeeGees records. Moved by the disco anthems, Brian picked up on a riff and David joined in with a beat. The next thing anybody knew, the band had a new song that everybody loved and nobody knew what to do with. The arguments against featuring the tune on *Follow the Leader* were many, but all were rooted in the same fear—the hard rocker's phobia of all things disco.

"I don't think we're going to put this on the record. This is an instrumental song."

"I don't know, man. I don't know if we should put this on the record. People are gonna be like, 'You fucking pussies.' "

Eventually, reason prevailed. "We weren't sure if we were gonna keep it," recounted Jonathan, "we were just kind of testing it out, playing it for friends, and it always ended up being everybody's favorite song." That was all the rationale the band needed to put some of their vocalist's angsty words to the song and record it for the album. In several months, Korn would spit in the face of their fear, going so far as to choose this hands-down fave as the lead single.

There were also those studio time–saving epiphanies when the band realized that songs once left in the discard pile were now worthy for inclusion on *Follow the Leader*. "My Gift to You" stands out as the most obvious example. The song had been written years before Korn was so much as a kernel in Fieldy's eye. Munky, Fieldy, and David had worked it out while still playing under the auspices of LAPD, but thought better of including it on their next album, *Korn*. They had, in fact, played it a few times after Jonathan's conscription some five years ago. At the time, however, they were not prepared to remove it from the reject bin.

One day, while working on the new CD, the group was stir-crazy. Bored and looking to blow off steam, they launched into a rendition of "My Gift to You" as a joke, only to hear the room erupt in a round of approbation. After beefing up the chorus into the "heaviest" thing they'd ever written, the guys were ready to hand their handiwork over to the resident lyricist.

With the pre-production process slated to last indefinitely, Jonathan had no need to engage in any more marathon songwriting sessions. Writing lyrics in his own good time allowed him the freedom to wait for inspiration. With "My Gift to You" the stimulus came from a most unlikely muse, a woman for whom he'd yet to write so much as a single verse: his girlfriend Renée. Although she'd always wanted to get a love song out of her reticent fiancé, Jonathan had always saved his aggro messages for the women on his shit list. Not this time.

The words to "My Gift to You," Jonathan said, are "about me wanting to kill my chick while I'm fucking her. It's about me choking her out while I'm banging her. It's just a sick fantasy I've always had. Just to be able to see through her eyes, to see if I could feel myself. To see if I could feel what it feels like to get nailed by me—all kinds of stuff. That's the weirdest song I ever wrote."

Needless to add, the singer's relationship with the mother of his child leaned toward the unconventional. Indeed, Jonathan's morbid fascination with death paled in comparison to Renée's, who'd been known to leave love letters on his pillow, delineating the multifarious ways in which she'd have liked to see him die. Still, even this mistress of the dark was taken aback by the gruesome expression of Jonathan's undying love.

"Thank you, that's kinda fucked up," she told him. "I was expecting a fuckin' 'I love you, baby' kinda song."

"No, you know me," replied Jonathan.

Indeed, Renée did know her boyfriend. Whatever imagery the lyrics might one day spark in the mind of little Nathan, the song went over great in the Davis household. Another track certain to start the blood curdling is "Pretty." But whereas "My Gift to You" had been the result of a death fantasy, the lyrics to "Pretty" stemmed from a death nightmare. The recollection of his nights at the morgue had never left the singer. Still beset by memories he'd have just as soon blocked out, Jonathan decided to take the most horrifically vivid and commit them to paper.

On Korn's first album, he'd tried writing about the baby girl who'd been brought into the coroner's after being raped by her father, but the words wouldn't come. After having a child of his own, however, the power of the haunting image intensified. "All the kid shit from the coroner's office started fucking with me. I'd chop up babies all the time. Seeing little Sarina, seeing Nathan—those were people I was fucking hacking up like a piece of meat. That shit fucks me up. I had a dream about it one night, and I was thinking about it, and the song just came out."

No doubt Jonathan owed many of these nightmares to the influence of his father. By discouraging his musical aspirations, Rick Davis had unwittingly led his son straight to death's door. "Dead Bodies Everywhere" would be Jonathan's take on the "parents just don't understand" anthem. "That song is about me wanting to get into the music business, but my dad wanted it to be something else," he elaborated. "So I ended up working at the coroner's office, with dead bodies everywhere. And that fucked my head up forever."

Death came up once again with the penning of "Justin." While one could extrapolate, the lyrics dealt almost exclusively with the band's experience with a terminally ill boy. When the Make-A-Wish Foundation apprised Korn of the fourteen-year-old's losing battle with colon cancer, and asked them to make his wish come true by paying him a visit, Jonathan had a crisis of the most existential variety. "I truly just freaked out," he attested. "It's like, 'Why would you want to meet me? What makes me so special?' And in turn I talk about how I admire his strength and his life." In the end, Korn wound up spending days with the ailing teen. "We got so attached to this kid," Jonathan said, "totally forgot he was gonna die."

Since the songwriter usually found his voice at moments of acute distress it is perhaps surprising that "Seed" was an ode to the innocence he saw in his son. But even this sweet message was not without its dark overtones, as Jonathan focused primarily on contrasting his son's cherubic life to his own harried existence. Like "Got the Life," "B.B.K.," and "Freak on a Leash," "Seed" revolved around the mixed blessings of fame.

Walking around stressed and pressed for time bore no resemblance to the "sex, drugs, and rock 'n' roll" fantasy that Korn had envisioned during their days as young dreamers. And yet, here they were, trying desperately to come up with an album that would take their sound in a new direction without discrediting them as bar-coded sellouts to their hardcore constituency.

Although recruiting a cast of guest stars to rival a Puff Daddy joint might not have been the best way to reassert their fealty to the underground, Korn could not thumb their proverbial nose at the chance to work with some of their best friends and favorite performers. Anyway, how long could a two-time Grammy nominee with a fan base more than two million strong keep harping on their subterraneous stature without beginning to sound ridiculous?

With the dawning of 1998, the band netted their second Grammy nod for Best Metal Performance, for "No Place to Hide" from their platinum-plated album, *Life Is Peachy*. Pantera's "Cemetery Gates," Tool's "Aenema," Corrosion of Conformity's "Drowning in a Daydream," and Megadeth's "Trust" accounted for the rest of the contenders. From Korn's prior touring experiences, one might surmise that the guys did not wish to win so much as they wanted Megadeth's Dave Mustaine to lose. Although Korn would ultimately be passed over for the Grammy, they could take solace in the fact that the jewel of the recording artists' crown had gone to Tool. Some eight months prior, David had himself expressed his admiration for the 1998 Best Metal Performance winners, saying, "I haven't actually listened to [The *Aenema* album] yet, but just hearing a few songs from friends, I like what I've heard."

Despite the loss, a second nomination—not to mention their own record company and a recently announced tour package entitled Family Values—testified to Korn's klout in the music industry and ushered in what many would soon term "The Year of the Korn." And with Jonathan spending so much of his tortured-artist-at-work time ruminating upon the drawbacks of fame, it was high time that the band began to enjoy all the advantages that came with a high profile. To wit, guest appearances from Ice Cube, Pharcyde's Tré Hardson, and Cypress Hill's B-Real were swiftly arranged.

Korn found a track ideally suited to Ice Cube's rapping in Fieldy's composition, "Fieldy's Dream." With the help of a drum machine, Fieldy had the rhythm section all laid out. After Munky and Head cut their guitar parts, the track was put aside. Once Ice Cube agreed to lend his talents, "Fieldy's Dream" quickly became "Children of the Korn." According to Fieldy, the no-nonsense rapper did not mess around in the studio. He came prepared and

conducted himself like a consummate professional until
the track was done. While Jonathan made a good show of
matching Cube's equanimity, his calm expression belied a
heart that was leaping for joy. "He's like my idol. I fucking love him," he gushed. "I was so scared to sing with
him because he's like the one guy in hip-hop I respect.
I've kind of lost it for hip-hop now, but old-school—I love
that shit. Him in N.W.A., and then him sitting there singing with me; I was freaking the fuck out. Like, singing
with your favorite artist ever."

Judging by the other guests to grace Korn's studio, Ice
Cube was not the only hip-hop artist Jonathan admired.
Tré provided "Cameltosis" with a dose of Pharcyde rhyme
and syncopation when he ventured into the Korn fray.
Hanging out in the studio, he began to improvise a rap
about women just as Jonathan was ready to take a torch
to the whole gender. "I was pissed off at women—women
who will rip your fucking heart out and feed it to you . . .
well, just one woman who wanted to fuck me up," Jonathan recalled. "I just heard [Tré] say something about
love, and I was like, 'Ah, okay, I'm gonna fuck this up
right now.' And I went for it, and it just took off from
there."

Indeed, the rapped verses of "Cameltosis" boasted the
same heavy backbeat as *Follow the Leader*'s other hip-hop-
centered track, "Children of the Korn." The group
planned to endow their collaboration with Cypress Hill's
B-Real with the same fat instrumental tracks. But getting
B-Real into the recording studio would prove easier said
than done. For weeks the band had waited for Cypress
Hill's label, Ruffhouse Records, to clear the long-overdue
guest appearance. When the record company finally came
back with a "Sorry, try again," Korn were left without
much lead time to find a replacement.

Enter Fred Durst, Limp Bizkit's inimitable frontman.

Touring with Korn, as well as a veritable parade of other well-known rockers, Limp Bizkit were gaining a mass following and their 1997 debut, *Three Dollar Bill, Y'All$*, was beginning to shift tonnage. While many of Korn's faithful had been loath to open their hearts to the rap-metal quintet, citing Bizkit's undue resemblance to Korn as the reason, Fieldy, Jonathan, David, Munky and Head couldn't have been any more supportive of the outfit. The groups had bonded over their innumerable roadside escapades, one of which Durst has yet to live down. "We were touring with Korn, and I'd spent all my money," he recalled. "Korn bet me five hundred dollars that I wouldn't sing 'Faith' naked. So 'Faith' came up, and I ran to the side of the stage and stripped buck-naked, except for my Kangol hat and my Adidas shoes. I was not at my most proud naked moment. Next thing you know, I'm looking on the Internet and there's a picture of it. But I got five hundred bucks!"

Durst's long-running relationship with Korn made him the perfect substitute for B-Real. As an added bonus, the joint venture was also bound to go a long way toward clearing up any misconceptions Korn fans might have had of the Bizkit as so-called Korn rip-off. Further evidence of the friendly rapport between the two groups came on an early installment of the *Korn After-School Special*. By implementing a "Korn TV" department on their official Web site in March 1998, the band had accomplished the unprecedented feat of milking the Internet for all its much-touted, but little-tapped worth. Using RealMedia software, any fan with a high-speed modem connection and an hour to spare could watch his or her favorite band going about the business of recording *Follow the Leader* or kicking it with studio guests such as Limp Bizkit.

After the Bizkit's stint on the *Korn After-School Special* came to an end, Jonathan and Fred Durst retired to the studio to brainstorm a concept for the track that would be "All in the Family." The result of this meeting of the minds would be *Follow the Leader*'s version of "K@#ø%!"—a song created with the express purpose of getting teens across America all hot and bothered. According to Jonathan, the two singers were equally enthused about the notion of bagging on each other to "make kids freak out and call each other up on the phone, and say, 'Ah, fuck—did you hear that shit?' "

With this goal in mind, the guys retreated into opposite corners of the studio to jot down their vocal parts. They bagged the track that very night. To everyone's immense satisfaction, "All in the Family" turned out to be a song after Korn's own heart. From that point on, no one who passed the studio's threshold was allowed to leave without hearing Jonathan and Fred's word fight. In fact, Fieldy has been known to claim that they played it for so many of their friends that he can no longer listen to it "unless there's someone in the car who hasn't heard it yet."

Once instituted, the weekly *Korn After-School Special* cybercasts took off with the help of appearances from musical guests such as Limp Bizkit, Sugar Ray, Deftones, 311, Pharcyde, and the champion of the seven-string, Steve Vai. Syndicated funnymen such as *Loveline*'s Adam Corrolla and *What's Happening*'s Fred "Rerun" Berry were also on hand to infuse the *Special* with some brandname humor. Last but not least, Korn's warped vision of a variety show would not have been complete without a regular who's who of porn stars and smut peddlers. "Fuck it, I like porn," Jonathan admitted. "I don't give a fuck. I have a huge-ass collection, 'bout a hundred movies. I love fuckin' sex. I love it, I love it, I love it. I like raunchy porn—the nastier, the better."

After witnessing the wanton goings-on at Kamp Korn, Epic Records executives had a fit. Fornicators, pornographers, and Adam Corolla, oh my . . . This was no laughing matter. Thoughts of lawsuits and Mothers Against Korn unions had the label in a panic. Unfortunately for Epic, their frantic pleas fell on deaf ears. All appeals to the musicians' better judgment were greeted by the same response: "Don't tell us what to do."

To Korn's way of thinking, the live show was nothing less than a stroke of genius, a brilliant extension of their gold (going on platinum) *Who Then Now?* home video. "It was cool because we had no censorship, so we just went balls-out," Jonathan recalled fondly. "We had such a fun time doing the *Korn After-School Special* shows. It's just a window for our fans to see what we do, to see us recording and other stuff, and to keep their interest. That's why we do that show. They get to see what we do. They'd get to see us in the studio, and we'd take phone calls from fans, and we'd have musical guests . . . and then we'd have that fun shit. It was all good."

The series' most memorable episode, however, did not involved anyone named Cherry or Bambi. The guys had been laying the groundwork for their biggest cybercast for days before the big unveiling. It all began one night at the studio, after Munky and David had left for their respective domiciles. The three remaining band members were loitering about when Fieldy piped up with an idea.

"How about that Cheech and Chong song?" he offered.

As fate would have it, one of the studio technicians just happened to have a copy of the 1978 *Up In Smoke* soundtrack languishing in his glove compartment. After popping the tape into the cassette player, the guys realized that "Earache My Eye"—the song to which Fieldy had been referring—did sound an awful lot like a seminal

Korn tune. In any case, the trio were just drunk enough to try it.

"Jon, get on the drums," Fieldy directed, as he headed for the mike.

With Brian filling in on guitar, the guys played for seven hours before calling it a night. "The next day," recounted Fieldy, "we woke up and I had no voice and Jon couldn't move because he's not used to playing drums. I had to take him to the chiropractor."

The marathon jam session not only left the threesome with a new respect for their bandmates, but a new track as well. But Korn's cover of "Earache My Eye" might never have made it onto *Follow the Leader* had the guys not followed through on their morning-after inspiration. "God, we should get ahold of Cheech," they said, not daring to believe that the comedic legend would actually find room enough in his schedule to comply.

Unwilling to wallow in uncertainty for so much as another day, the guys called their manager pronto. "We asked our manager to call Cheech's office and ask him if he wanted to come down and do 'Earache My Eye,' " recounted Jonathan.

Soon they had their answer.

"Yeah, he's here in town," relayed Korn's manager, "and yeah, he'd love to do it."

Within a matter of days, Cheech Marin had materialized in the lounge of NRG Recording Studios, and Korn fans nationwide were logging on to their computers to watch this very special *Korn After-School Special*. While "Earache My Eye" would be *Follow the Leader*'s secret bonus track, the guys made no secret of their recording process, cutting the track before the very eyes of their cyber-savvy fan base. Lead vocals were sung by Fieldy and, of course, Cheech Marin himself, the drums were manned by Jonathan, David played the bass guitar, and Brian and Munky swapped guitar parts. The end result was the epitome of puerile fun, and definitely a Korn song.

Lest readers walk away with the impression that recording *Follow the Leader* went smoothly for the kings of the road, they need only think back to the great T-shirt imbroglio to be reminded of the various distractions that plagued and extended the band's production schedule. While the guys were toiling away in their North Hollywood recording studio, trouble was brewing some two thousand miles to the northeast.

It all began innocently enough on a crisp winter's morning. On March 5, 1998, Eric VanHoven, an eighteen-year-old high-school junior, was readying himself for another day of classes at Michigan's Zeeland High School. Without stopping to think, he threw on his old Korn T-shirt and headed out the door. Within hours of his arrival, however, he was sitting in Assistant Principal Gretchen Plewes's office and listening as she lambasted him for committing acts unbecoming to a Zeeland High student. Now Eric would have to face the music: one day's suspension.

What had he done to deserve this censure? He'd ventured to wear a Korn T-shirt—the very shirt that he'd worn to school on countless other occasions. But for the Korn logo, the T-shirt boasted no identifying characteristics. Still, according to Assistant Principal Plewes, this was an outrage all in itself. "The group called Korn is one of three groups that I'm familiar with that have extremely offensive lyrics," she told the local newspaper. "Korn is indecent, vulgar, obscene, and intends to be insulting. It is no different than a person wearing a middle finger on their shirt."

When the newswires and MTV got wind of the story, Korn became front-page news, and high-school students all over America joined in their disapproval of Zeeland High School's authoritarian regime. The Monday after the well-publicized suspension, Zeeland High students started circulating an anti–dress code petition and putting what they'd learned of Thoreau's lessons in civil disobedience into action. Namely, VanHoven and ten of his friends showed up at school wearing T-shirts bearing the names of bands such as Tool, Filter and Nirvana—VanHoven's best friend even risked suspension by donning a Korn T-shirt. As expected, the Tool logo–sporting VanHoven and his Korn-klad best friend both found themselves suspended. Clearly the words "free country" meant little to the assistant principal.

While Eric VanHoven might not have expected Korn to come to his rescue, the band did exactly that. When word of the fracas reached the balmy shores of L.A., the guys tore themselves away from their album long enough to talk to their lawyers.

"We just thought it was ridiculous, beyond ridiculous," Fieldy later asserted. "It's like, 'What the fuck—what's this world coming to? You can't wear a shirt that has a name on it?' I can understand if it said 'fuck' or something like that, but it was like saying 'Korn' is like saying 'fuck' or 'shit.' "

In response to the assistant principal's admonitions, the band demonstrated that hell hath no fury like Korn scorned. After teleconferencing with their lawyers and managers, the group issued a statement denouncing Assistant Principal Gretchen Plewes's moralizing. Going still further, they slapped the school district with a cease-and-desist order, instructing the assistant principal to either abstain from making any more defamatory comments about their band, or to prepare for a multi-million-dollar lawsuit. And as if that was not bad enough, the group then commissioned the production of five hundred Korn T-shirts with the First Amendment and the words "Except in Michigan" printed on the back, and dispatched the lot to Zeeland High. "We contacted the local radio station and they took the T-shirts down to the school," recalled Jonathan, clearly relishing the memory. "They said that the cops were there because they thought there was going to be a riot. But it ended up that all the cops handed out all the Korn T-shirts to the kids. It was awesome."

While all's well that ends with Korn getting extra mileage out of their detractors, the disruptive T-shirt controversy was obviously one distraction that the studio-wan band could have done without. But insofar as it related to the group's recording process, the problem was minor in comparison to the total confusion that descended upon the guys when they got their first mixes back from producer Steve Thompson. The songs did not sound like Korn—something was off. But what to do about it, that was the million-dollar question. At first, the musicians did nothing but scratch their heads in puzzlement. As Jonathan explained, "It sounded foreign to us, not right, but we were all used to hearing shitty music."

Finally, they came to the unanimous conclusion that for all his success and distinction, Steve Thompson was not the producer for Korn. At this point, Thompson had already put in four months at the boards—a long time, but certainly not past the point of no return. With the quality of the album at stake, the guys handed the producer's reins to their sound engineer, Toby Wright. For weeks after the change in leadership, chaos reigned supreme. When all the chinks were ironed out, however, the new studio chief proved to be an overwhelming improvement. "Hearing the album now, and the change we made, it was all worth it," confirmed Jonathan. "Now that

I hear it, it's 'Oh my god!' I'm glad we made the change. It was good for us and we deserved it."

Before the album was so much as sequenced, the guys were already waxing rhapsodic on the subject of its sundry artistic merits. Everything they'd set out to accomplish as a band could be glimpsed on *Follow the Leader.* "We put those other two CDs on compared to this one, and it's night and day," claimed Fieldy. "Our other two records sound like demos."

The production was flawless, but were fans going to like the music? Would *Follow the Leader*, with all its special effects and in-studio wizardry, go down as the album that topped the *Korn* standard? Nine months of work, an illustrious list of guest stars, a $500,000 budget, and some $20,000 worth of Coors Light and Jack Daniel's said that it would. But in the first week of June 1998—just days after Fieldy bit the bullet and married Shela, the mother of his eight-month-old daughter—Korn was still nearly three months shy of learning the final verdict.

10
a korner on the market

Lately it had seemed as though every few months brought either a wedding, a birth, or some other bit of good tidings. And the streak would only grow longer; like moths to a flame, the festive occasions would keep on cropping up within the realm of Korn. The latest event to rock Korn's world would be the birth of Head's baby, Jennea-Marie Welch. Whatever travel-induced problems the guitarist and his girlfriend Rebekkah may have had in the past, their recent wedding ceremony proved that love had indeed conquered all.

Putting family before work must have figured prominently into the compromise struck by the newly married Welches. Evidence of Brian's priority roster surfaced when Korn had to cancel their single Ozzfest engagement. The power bill for the June 20 show at the U.K.'s Milton Keynes Bowl also featured Black Sabbath, Foo Fighters, Pantera, and Slayer. Metal fans had to reconcile themselves to this four-act lineup, as the concert conflicted with Rebekkah's due date. In their second display of solidarity since the Lollapalooza resignation, the rest of Korn declined to participate in the event without Head.

But while Ozzfest's sole European engagement went on as planned, Rebekkah's pregnancy exceeded its plotted nine-month course by more than two weeks. At length, the baby had to be delivered by way of induced labor on July 6, 1998—making Head a proud father, and Munky the last of the swinging singles on the tour bus.

This shift in the group dynamic marked the beginning of a new Korn. The band that had fought tooth and nail to climb to the top, touring relentlessly for years and taking breaks only to record albums and enjoy a quick Christmas dinner, was finally running out of energy. With their familial obligations and soaring popularity, it was time to admit victory. The group was ready to move on to grander ventures that required less stamina and brute force and more planning and coordination. "We're not gonna tour our asses off like we did last time," Fieldy predicted. "It was really hard. I remember one of the bus drivers saying it was the hardest tour he'd been on in twenty years... We toured hard, like a day off every two weeks. Nobody does that. But I don't regret it, 'cause we broke."

For Korn, the next level of touring would be defined by the Family Values tour package. Plans for the tour had been under way ever since Korn had bowed out of Lollapalooza a year before. While the band had, at the time, expressed an appreciation for the variety of styles and genres represented by Lolla, their true feelings were that the festival had spread itself too thin. The accuracy of Korn's opinion was reflected in Lolla's floundering ticket sales, which had fallen far short of such focused outings as Ozzfest, Lilith Fair, and the Warped tour.

At Family Values, fans could expect to enjoy five full hours of nothing but the heaviest in modern rock music. "With Family Values," explained Fieldy, "we don't want to have too much of a mix-up. You've got to keep it kind of the same vibe. Like, Lollapalooza was just too mixed up, man. Like, Tricky and Ziggy Marley, and then Korn and Tool. It just doesn't make sense. You want everybody to like every band and have a good time the whole time."

The plan sounded simple enough, but finding like-minded bands turned out to be more of a problem than Korn had originally anticipated. Orgy, whose *Candyass* CD was scheduled for release at the same time as *Follow the Leader*, had been the first act to come on board. Limp Bizkit soon followed suit. But as Fieldy would later explain, this triumvirate was still "not enough for a festival." The band that Korn wanted most of all were the Deftones. The long-standing friendship between the two groups would have made for an ideal touring experience, but the Deftones had other, presumably more important issues to sort out—they absolutely refused to go on before Limp Bizkit.

"We asked them, almost to the point of begging them, many times, to be on Family Values because we're friends with them and we would have had a good time hanging out every night," Fieldy later explained. "But they said no and they took a bullshit tour that they're hating right now. They were playing stupid like, 'We're not going on before Limp Bizkit.' Who cares when who goes on? I'm sure if we talked to Limp Bizkit they'd switch slots, I told them that. We're trying to make a family thing and have a good time. But their managers talked some shit into their heads. Whatever. They're missing out on what's gonna be the funnest tour of all time."

In all matters that relate to package tours, and the entertainment industry in general, managers are usually the ones to bear the brunt of responsibility for their clients' decisions—especially when those decisions go awry. The Korn versus Rob Zombie melee was no different. Rob Zombie and Ice Cube had been signed to complete the Family Values tree in the spring of 1998. While a rapper might not have qualified as a heavy act, Fieldy defended the decision by saying, "I think all our fans really like hip-hop. We're really close to our fans. We talk to them all the time, and all the fans we've ever talked to are into hip-hop because they know—look at the way we dress."

Sure enough, with two rap-metal acts gracing the bill, a purely hip-hop-oriented show, such as Ice Cube's, and a metal one, such as Rob Zombie's, would have served to anchor the festival. This happy outcome, however, was not to be. The first sign that all was not going as planned came in July, in the form of a press release proclaiming that the Family Values tour would be substituting Rob Zombie with German industrialists Rammstein. "We just heard about them," Jonathan said of Rammstein. "I first heard them in that David Lynch film *Lost Highway*. They're like, blowing up now, like the new Ministry. We thought it would be better for Family Values, since they're up-and-coming and all that. And they don't even speak English and stuff, so that's gonna be fun, too. And that fuck sets himself on fire. It's just gonna be a good time."

Okay, but what of Rob Zombie? According to Korn's management, the reasons for Zombie's departure were threefold. First was his reluctance to play alongside a hip-hop artist, which manifested itself in repeated lectures on why "rock kids don't like hip-hop." Second was the fact that the Family Values tour promoters had not calculated on the fact that Zombie would be going on solo instead of performing with the whole of his band, White Zombie. And lastly, they claimed that Zombie's desired stage setup was too elaborate for a package show. Of all these explanations, Rob Zombie concurred only with the latter.

In fact, it was his contention that Korn's management had known all along that he was going to perform sans White Zombie to support his forthcoming *Hellbilly Deluxe* solo album. What's more, he insisted that not only was he not averse to touring with Ice Cube, but that he owned several of the rapper's albums and considered him to be the best part of the whole lineup. The only reason he'd given for leaving the tour was his elaborate stage design. "You can't build a huge den of Satan and tear it down in five minutes. It's just not possible," he reaffirmed. "I thought they'd understand. Then, like four or five days later, there's this press release with these crazy statements making it sound like they came from me, and I never spoke to them. They're just milking it for publicity, I guess. What else is new?"

Not one to run from a skirmish, Zombie explained that he called Jeff Kwatinetz, Korn's manager and the co-organizer of Family Values, as soon as he heard about the allegations.

"What is this press release? What, are you out of your mind?" he stormed.

"It doesn't come across like that," replied Kwantinetz.

"What do you mean, it doesn't come across like that?" demanded Zombie. "Why am I on the phone with *Time* magazine if it doesn't come across like that?"

Oddly enough, *Time* magazine was actually interested in the scuffle, running a short piece under the headline "Family Circus" and referring to the tour as having reached "a Faulknerian level of dysfunction." If Korn's management firm had set out to attract publicity, they'd emerged victorious. But the musicians themselves might not have fared so well in the war of the managerial teams. The spin-doctoring of the managers and tour organizers left Korn in the crossfire, unable to distinguish truth from fiction. Jonathan chalked the mishap up to Zombie's manager, saying, "Our band has nothing against Rob, but his manager . . . was trying to have creative control of our tour." Meanwhile, Fieldy maintained that it was Zombie himself who was "acting like a rock-star dickhead, wanting to control everything."

While *Time* magazine had concluded their article with the words, "Don't wait for a Family Reunion tour," the truth of the matter was that Rob Zombie held no grudge against the members of Korn. His beef was with the tour organizers, not the band. "I don't even know those guys," he said, "so I need to meet them before I can feud with them." Within six months of the Family Values tour, Korn and Rob Zombie would finally have a chance to meet—but, despite *Time*'s prophecies of doom, feuding would not figure into the agenda.

Although the Family Values shuttle wasn't scheduled to blast off until mid-September, Korn didn't intend to wait for fall to promote *Follow the Leader*. For all their declarations of loyalty to the subterranean scene, the guys wanted nothing so much as to hear the sound of their CD blaring out of every subway commuter's headphones, every beachfront boom box, and every home stereo system. "You know, the main reason we're making music is to let people hear it," confirmed Fieldy. "It's like, we want the whole world to hear what we're doing, everyone."

A number one album would certainly go a long way toward fulfilling that Everyrocker's fantasy. But given the checkered nature of Korn's past relationship with MTV, debuting atop the *Billboard* 200 would be no mean feat. Necessity being the mother of invention, the band quickly came up with a backup plan. Whether or not MTV proved consistent in their lack of support, the group would do what they'd always done to get ahead—tour.

But Korn Kampaign '98 would be more like a political campaign than an ordinary promotional tour. To generate interest in the August 18 release of *Follow the Leader*, the guys would take their message to the streets of America starting August 17. Stopping just short of kissing babies and petting puppies, they'd charter their own jet, hit some fifteen record stores across the nation and hold fun-filled fan-ferences at each and every site. Like all of Korn's precedent-setting ideas, this one was pure marketing genius.

In July 1998, the band's management was booking appearances around the clock, but there was still no word on the type of reception Korn could expect from MTV. The question mark hanging over the group's aspirations to the mainstream would turn to vapor by month's end. After agreeing to cast "Got the Life" in the role of lead single, the group sent it out to radio on July 24. While the guys had been considering the possibility of not shooting a video for the song, their plans were foiled when "Got the Life" became the most-added track to alternative and rock radio stations' playlists. At that point, not only did MTV assign special correspondent John Norris to cover the ins and outs of the Korn Kampaign, but as Jonathan explained, "MTV is now begging us for a video. So we're doing a video. What the heck, all it can do is help us. It can't hurt us. We'll give it to them and see what happens. We'll see if they finally give us some love."

The videotaping would have to wait a week, as Korn were due to perform before 67,000 music fans at Japan's Fuji Rock Festival on August 2—their first live show since Lollapalooza. With Garbage, the Prodigy, Björk, Beck, Elvis Costello, and Ben Folds Five all scheduled to play, the event was a veritable invitation into the mainstream. After alighting in Tokyo, however, the guys felt more like gate-crashers than VIPs. It seems that other bands didn't take too kindly to Korn's particular brand of good-natured ribbing. Take, for instance, Jonathan's musings on the sonic stylings of Ben Folds Five: "Goddamn Ben Folds Five sucks. It's fucking *Cheers* music." Neither did Fieldy's attempts at bonding with Garbage's Shirley Manson (by repeatedly sticking a noise-emitting keychain in her face) go over too well.

The bad-boy reputation inspired by these admittedly repellent antics left the group feeling unloved and misunderstood. But, according to Jonathan, this was nothing out of the ordinary. One drunken evening, he related the pain of the band's wretched plight, proving once and for all that naughty boys need love, too. "We go to these goddamn festivals, and no fucking goddamn band will love us," he complained. "We get no fucking love at all. It's like we're in our own little world. We're not that goddamn scary. What the goddamn fuck? For once in my life, please love me: I'm in Korn."

While Jonathan's pleas would go unanswered, the band's acceptance issues were soon dwarfed by their enormous performance anxiety on the morning of the concert. Never before had the guys been away from the stage for such a long stretch. Jonathan had woken up at the crack of dawn to focus all of his faculties just on memorizing the lyrics to the songs; Head had been beset by nightmares; while Fieldy was oscillating between throwing up, swilling beer, and popping Xanax. While the performance itself incited the usually sedate Japanese crowds to lose their composure and break into an unruly mess of a mosh pit, the group insisted that they'd "sucked." The next day, Jonathan even suffered a panic attack and had to be tended to by the band's resident shrink.

All told, the Fuji Rock Festival witnessed a low point in Korn's career. Of course, it was one from which they'd rebound just as soon as they saw *Follow the Leader* perched atop the *Billboard* 200.

When the group touched down at LAX, they might well have kissed the ground for all the joy they felt at being home. Their legions of fans, their friends, and their families had all been awaiting their arrival. There was a video to be shot, interviews to be endured, advance album reviews to be read, and children to be comforted. Jonathan, for one, was eager to see his son, as the two had had a most unsatisfying parting before Korn set off for Tokyo. "It really freaked me out when I left to go to Japan and my son said, 'You got to go to work? 'Bye, Daddy.' Then he rolled over, like, 'Don't talk to me.' It hurt my feelings more than anything in the world."

While Head and David also had family matters to attend to, Fieldy's wife was five months pregnant with their second baby. In the spring, while Korn was still working on *Follow the Leader*, Fieldy had begun producing the eponymous album of Elementree's second band, Videodrone (the very band that had provided Jonathan with his first concertgoing experience, back when they were still known as Cradle of Thorns). By all accounts, the bassist had been having a tough time balancing the demands of career and family. "Fieldy went through a lot of shit when he was [producing Videodrone]," Brian recounted, "but he had to do it, he had to go after it. He didn't get to see his family a lot because he was working with us writing, and then afterwards, he'd go hang out with them and help them write songs the same day. He had a little girl, and one on the way, plus his wife . . . It was hard for him, but he got through it and did a good job." According to Kris Kohls, Videodrone's drummer, family time wasn't the only thing Fieldy missed out on. "He didn't get that much sleep between working on his band and us," said Kohls.

Bearing in mind the dizzying pace that would commence with the start of Korn Kampaign '98, the guys used the few free days they had left to play the dutiful husbands and fathers, as well as to shoot the video for "Got the Life." Not three weeks later, on Monday, August 17, they were in a limo headed for the first stop of their Kampaign at a Los Angeles Tower Records. Approaching the scene of the event, the group was struck by the sight of two thousand autograph-seekers who'd braved the L.A. freeways to meet and greet the Bakersfield Five at the appointed midnight hour.

The next day's fan conference at Riverside, California's, Mad Platter record store saw the haggard band members inwardly groaning at the prospect of repeating Monday night's performance. "I'm hoping for about a hundred people," said David, " 'cause last night we went through about two thousand kids and didn't get to bed until six this morning, so we're tired. If we can get about a hundred, a hundred and ten kids there, we'll be happy."

But galvanized by Korn's hit single, "Got the Life," the kids came out in droves, dashing the group's hopes for an understated reception. Undeterred by the mammoth crowd, the band once again made good on their promise to deliver much more than a run-of-the-mill autograph-signing session. "The regular in-store thing is really boring," explained Jonathan. "The kids come in, we sign their stuff, they leave, and that's all they get out of it. With the Korn Kampaign, it's like there's a couple of different stages . . . we have our fan conference where the kids get to actually ask us questions . . . plus we have Jim Rose and all our special guests that they get to hang out and, you know, ask questions. Then after all that's done, we get to sign their stuff and they get to go on their way, so it's like a whole big scene. It's a big event."

Tuesday night's guests included Ice Cube, Fred Durst, and comic-book legend Todd McFarlane, the creator of the animated series *Spawn*. The latter's presence related directly to *Follow the Leader*'s cover art, a chilling illustration of a little girl hopscotching her way off the edge of a cliff while a mass of kids looks on, presumably ready to follow her lead. Since Korn's change of stylistic direction as well as the album title had both stemmed from other musicians' attempts to cop their sound, McFarlane's depiction was a faithful representation of the band's message.

Korn would hit one more site in southern California before taking to their specially-chartered plane and flying to San Francisco. From there, the group would move on to pack houses in Seattle, Minneapolis, Milwaukee, Chicago, Detroit, Philadelphia, Boston, New York, Toronto, Atlanta, Dallas, and Phoenix before reaching their final destination, home sweet home, on September 1. Not to put too fine a point on it, but when all was said and done, they'd stayed on the Kampaign trail for sixteen days, visited fifteen stores, enjoyed a total of two days off, and signed some twenty thousand copies of *Follow the Leader.*

Yet we'll shed no tears for Korn. After all, what is two weeks' worth of work and a bad case of writer's cramp compared to a lifetime filled with memories of a number one album?

Even before MTV got their grubby little paws on Korn's "Got the Life" video, catapulting the song and the band to ubiquity by virtue of *Total Request Live*, many music critics were already doffing their hats for the band that had set the FM frequencies abuzz with the sound of unfettered fury. While much was made of the group's unusual decision to start the CD at the thirteenth track, leaving each of the first twelve slots to occupy five seconds with dead air, it was the music itself that got to *Rolling Stone* reviewer David Fricke, who gave the album four out of a possible five stars. "In *Follow the Leader*," he wrote, "vocalist Jonathan Davis, bassist Reggie 'Fieldy' Arvizu, guitarists James 'Munky' Shaffer and Brian 'Head' Welch, and drummer David Silveria have made an ideal record for those long, black days when all you can do is stand up and scream, 'What the fuck! What the fuck! What the fuck!' at bloody-murder volume."

Although *Rolling Stone* called *Follow the Leader* Korn's "best album," others in the mainstream media were content to reserve their praise. *Spin* magazine, for instance, gave the album seven out of ten points—passing, but just barely. The text of the review, however, was far more harsh than the quantitative rating. According to *Spin*, "Korn scare all the right people—critics and faculty—but resonance is only supposed to be a beginning, not an end in itself. They don't have to grow up, they don't have to achieve 'closure,' but if they're not going to make good records, what's the point of going through all of that therapy?"

Entertainment Weekly was yet another tiger that refused to change its anti-Korn stripes. Although *EW*'s final grade was a respectable, albeit lackluster B-minus, the wordage whistled a different tune: "On one level, the album doesn't disappoint. It's a big load of dumb fun," the critic began. Going on to lavish the band with an array of equally backhanded compliments, the review finally concluded with the words, "Consider this a mix of the comic, the disparate, and the desperate. If that's hardly innovative enough to rival the classics of metal, at least Korn's LP gives this once-stagnant style kernels of something new."

Whatever blows the critics leveled at *Follow the Leader*, each had fallen far short of the mark. Never having relied on the media's support so much as on their own arsenal of resources, Korn were the "untouchables" of metal. Proving the band could do no wrong in the eyes of young, heavy-rock fans, the album landed at *Billboard*'s coveted number one position on August 28, 1998, nudging the previous week's winner, Snoop Dogg, down to number 3, and leaving the champions of two weeks prior, the Beastie Boys, at number 2 for the second week in a row. For Korn, the sales figures were well-nigh unbelievable— 268,000 U.S. consumers had bought their album in its first week of release. "You know what, I'm just glad we didn't have to go up against the Beastie Boys or Snoop," said a pragmatic David, "because we would have been down."

Suddenly everyone wanted Korn's mugs gracing the covers of their magazines, and Korn videos playing on their music networks. MTV had even thrown "Got the Life" into the kind of frequent rotation usually enjoyed only by the Backstreet Boys. Soon the song was as much a staple of *Total Request Live* as it was of modern-rock radio. "Everything's getting bigger," mused Munky. "It's a bigger production, we're getting more airplay, we're getting played on MTV—a lot of things are happening for us that haven't happened before. People are starting to get it, starting to understand what it's all about."

Meanwhile, Orgy, whose LP *Candyass* had also been released on August 18, was benefiting from the trickle-down success theory. Korn's sudden explosion had cast a radioactive glow around their friends, neighbors, and tour companions. Its first week on the racks, the album sold 5,000 copies and debuted on *Billboard*'s "Heatseekers" chart at number 16. These numbers would only increase with the belated release of the band's first single, an incisive cover of New Order's "Blue Monday," and the coming of the Family Values tour.

The official launch of Korn's first annual Family Values extravaganza had been set for September 22. This being the band's first U.S. tour in over a year, anticipation was at an all-time high. Despite many of the older fans' contentions that *Follow the Leader*—like *Life Is Peachy* before

it and, for that matter, any album the group would con-
coct in the future—could never measure up to the awe-
inspiring maelstrom that was *Korn*, the group was hotter
than ever.

No sooner had the LP snagged *Billboard*'s premier slot,
than all eyes were on the band that Middle America loved
to hate. And no one was savoring the attention more than
the five perennially love-starved outcasts of the summer
festival circuit. Never again would they have to endure
the oppressive heat of an outdoor summer show or the
indifferent audiences that came with playing second fiddle
to a better-known metal band. Headlining their own
arena-bound package tour, with a group of their nearest
and dearest friends and protégés to support them, Korn
felt like just so many masters of the universe. To wit, they
quickly got up the cojones to brave an IRS audit, and to
send the following cheeky missive to a former vice president.

Dear Vice President Quayle,

It would be entirely inappropriate and remiss of
us to not extend a personal invitation to you and
your family to be on-hand at any one of the tour
stops on "The Family Values" trek (September 22–
November 1).

Since we believe it was you who brought the
phrase "family values" to all of our attention, this
tour is somewhat of a tribute to you.

We'd be honored if you could come out and enjoy
the sounds of Korn, Rammstein, and Ice Cube, not
to mention such artists as Limp Bizkit and Orgy.

Listen to what you have created and look what
you have wrought.

Sincerely,
KOЯN

P.S. "All Excess" passes will be included with your tickets.

In fact, the name of the tour had been inspired by the very Republican who probably *would* have spelled *corn* with a *k*. As Jonathan explained, "It's just sarcasm, basically. It's everything that we're not about or all these bands are about. . . . You know the politicians that always said, you know, 'you keep our good family values' and how, you know, 'rock 'n' roll and rap is just killing the youth' and all that crap. We just named it that, it was just like a big you-know-what to all of those people."

Faithful to the tradition of Lollapalooza, they planned to keep Family Values trucking for years, breaking new bands and fortifying the stronghold of heavy rock, be it rap-metal, funk-thrash, death-pop, or just plain old industrial. As early as the fall of 1998, the group was already conspiring to bring the Deftones onto Family Values '99. Like Perry Farrell, the guys were also considering taking a more entrepreneurial, hands-off approach by letting the next year's shows run without them. Korn's imprint, however, would always be felt by the concertgoers, for the quintet had no plans to relinquish the right to pick the bands performing on their tour.

All designs on the future were, of course, contingent upon the immediate success of the first Family Values outing. But to hear the participants tell it, the capacity crowds and sold-out pavilions were but a foregone conclusion. "It's just the right time in music," enthused Fred Durst. "It's the right time in 1998. It's the best way to end off the year with a big boom. It's gonna be out of control."

Since there had never been a tour quite like this before, an avalanche of press notices was devoted to the Family Values migration pattern. Much of the speculation revolved around the bands' high-end stage designs and the spectacular light shows. Family Values promised to provide fans with the ultimate concert experience, a show that boasted the variety of a festival and the grand-scale production of an arena rock concert. "It all goes back to when I was a kid," Jonathan related. "I can remember how excited I'd get when a major band was scheduled to play in my hometown arena. Everything about it was great—all the people, all the commotion, even the way the sound would echo off of the back walls. To me, that's what rock 'n' roll is still about. You just don't get that same feeling when you play in a club, or even when you play in front of a big crowd outside. Arenas are really special."

Brian concurred. "Outdoor shows are cool and everything," he conceded, "but sound travels everywhere and it's not as pumping. Blowing the roof off the place indoors is better."

With each act featuring their own special set, a revolving stage had to be erected at every venue. Larger-than-life statues, complicated backdrops, and a thirty-foot-tall toilet bowl were just some of the attractions dazzling the swarming audiences. "It's Korn's Family Values tour, but it's like everyone has full use of the stage," marveled Durst. "There's nothing up on the stage but your production. And it's gigantic. Everyone has a huge production. It's, like, pretty unheard-of, the first time in our generation for this to be happening to us. It's like a Macy's Thanksgiving Day Parade, and every float is phatter."

Clearly the Bakersfield Five were not your standard-issue prima donnas, fretting lest one of their opening acts should outshine their own performance. In fact, it was Korn's magnanimous attitude toward their co-headliners that revealed the double entendre implicit in the Family Values name. "All the people we brought on tour are our friends," Jonathan said, "they're the people we party with." When Incubus came in to replace Ice Cube, who had to shove off due to a prior engagement to star in *Three Kings* with George Clooney and Mark Wahlberg, the guys played the benevolent hosts, making sure the newest addition wanted for nothing. One day, the group noticed that members of Incubus were not getting any catering. They got on the phone, no questions asked, and demanded that the group get their three squares per diem. "If it costs us a little bit of money out of our pocket to have a band be happy, so it does," shrugged Fieldy. "We bring bands out that we like. It's not like some bands that bring somebody out for ticket sales. Family Values—it's a family."

At the beginning, the trek was every bit the traveling carnival its creators had wanted it to be. Hanging out with their friends morning, noon, and night, taking a day or two off after every three shows just to recuperate, flying home to see their wives and kids when time allowed, the group had every right to congratulate themselves for organizing the perfect tour.

Make that *almost* perfect. On October 8, the Phoenix, Arizona, show had had to be canceled due to the fact that both Jonathan and Fred Durst had come down with the flu. To make up the skipped date, Family Values was forced to cancel their Boise, Idaho, concert, since that arena was smaller than the one in Phoenix. Although this stunt could not have gone over well with the potato capital's Korn fans, the tour was still going strong.

Then, prior to the festival's arrival at Louisiana's Cajundome, a local reverend and his church group voiced the concerns of parents all across America when they entered the venue and prayed for a "sense of protection." As always, Korn laughed in the face of such Bible-thumpers' meddling. But while thousands upon thousands of fans would keep right on pouring in, the good cheer would not last for the duration of the voyage.

While the pressure to get to the top had abated, it was immediately supplanted by the fear of slipping to the bottom. The unexpected stress that came with blatant mainstream recognition, often had the guys lunging for each other's throats. "Honestly, Family Values killed us. *Follow the Leader* came out, and we're getting accepted now, and all this fame or whatever was coming into our lives, and it really tore the band apart. It tore us up," Jonathan admitted. "Because we've always taken it a level at a time, and it's always [like this]. We go through our phases where the band's all torn up and everything because we're just trying to deal with all of this. It's so much coming down on you, all the fame and everything. You guys are embracing us now and everybody's coming to the party now."

With their tour muscles weakened by an extended stay in the studio, the guys were uncharacteristically wearied by the weeks spent on the road. While this tour was a pleasure cruise in comparison to their past excursions, the last days of the six-week jaunt witnessed Munky and Fieldy hanging on by very thin threads. In fact, according to Head, "Fieldy went crazy. He was getting ready to have his second child, and toward the end he was going crazy, yelling at people and stuff. And Munky . . . I don't know, they were going a little crazy, like they needed a break or something."

As it turned out, the one-and-a-half-month break in which Korn would indulge after their tour, was one they could well afford. From its inaugural September 22 stop in Rochester, New York, all the way to its October 31 farewell performance in Fairfax, Virginia—where to commemorate All Hallow's Eve, Limp Bizkit donned Elvis regalia, Korn paid an homage to eighties hair-band chic,

and most of Rammstein eschewed clothing altogether—
the tour drew massive numbers. Stopping only at the biggest and brightest venues such as L.A.'s Forum, San Francisco's Cow Palace, and Chicago's Rosemont Horizon, the
twenty-seven shows grossed a total that topped the $6.4
million mark, and cemented Korn's reputation as the leaders of the New Metal revolution. Not four months after
the final tour date, Orgy was a familiar sight on MTV,
Rammstein's unforgettable "Du Hast" video was finally
seeing the light of day, even if only on The Box, Limp
Bizkit's "Faith" was everywhere, and the video for Korn's
second single was second only to 'N Sync's insipid whin-
ing on *Total Request Live*. Politicians can say what they
will, but as Korn proved, Family Values are alive and well
in America.

Before they could enjoy their well-deserved breather,
Korn would have sacrificed three more weeks to the gods
of the open road. On November 2, the guys set off for
their own headlining tour, with Orgy as their opening act.
Scheduled to run through November 21, the tour got off
to a false start, and underscored the beleaguered outfit's
need for a respite, when Jonathan collapsed from exhaustion shortly after the second night's performance at Can-
ada's University of Montreal. That meant either canceling
the next evening's concert in Albany, New York, and resuming the tour two days later in Amherst, Massachu-
setts, or crossing their fingers in the hope that Jonathan
would not keel over once and for all. Not ones to put their
trust in faith-healing, Korn took no chances, opting out
of the Albany performance.

The musicians picked up where they left off on November 6 and continued felling arena after coliseum unim-
peded, until their grand finale in Nashville's Municipal
Auditorium. No doubt, by this time each of the group's

five uneasy pieces were thinking something along the lines of, "There's no place like home."

The band arranged to be back on the road come 1999. The holiday season ahead, however, wasn't fallow even by a rock star's standards. November was a red-letter month if only because of Jonathan's painstakingly concocted wedding ceremony. The fun began with a no-expense-spared bachelor party. With a mind to expand upon the whips, chains, and strippers motif of his twenty-seventh birthday blowout, Jonathan invited porn magnate Matt Zane to throw his last hurrah.

The creative force behind such triple-X-classics as *House of Flesh 1* and *2* as well as *Backstage Sluts 1* and *2* Zane had long been a friend after Jonathan's own heart. "He does fresh, new shit," raved the vocalist. "Reverse gang bangs where this guy gets fucked by eighteen chicks. He adds action shit in his movies, stunts and shit." With such an adept organizer, the fiesta was certain to be nothing if not festive. Besides essentials such as a dominatrix and a she-male, the bachelor bash included "a little skinny girl and big fat girl who put a double dong in between each other," Jonathan reminisced. "Then there was, like, an eight-girl orgy, and I was right in the middle."

Well aware of her fiancé's penchant for porn, Renée had always taken a "boys will be boys" approach to Jonathan's frequent trips to the ALL NUDE GIRLS part of town. So instead of giving rise to a disconsolate bride and a custody battle, the bachelor party was followed by a wedding that Jonathan described as "just awesome." Apparently, Renée's idea had been to steep the ceremony in medieval tradition. With a castle, knights in shining armor, fairies in flowing gowns, and enough sprites and elves to populate an enchanted forest, the event provided a marked contrast to Jonathan's brooding public persona. Afterward, the couple set off for their honeymoon, leaving the rest of the kernels to tend their own gardens.

With Shela Arvizu's due date just days away, Fieldy's home grounds were especially fertile. Making up for lost time, the bass player spent most of his vacation catering to his rotund wife's every craving. The wait ended in December, when Shela gave birth to their second daughter, Olivia. For now, Fieldy's brood was the largest of the Korn field. But with Shannon Silveria two months pregnant, this distinction was bound to be short-lived.

With the holidays at an end, it was right back to work for the five revitalized musicmen. Ever since the release of *Follow the Leader* and the resounding success of the Family Values tour, Korn had segued from the manse of mere rock-stardom into the pantheon of living legends. An institution in their own right, the guys were invited to open 1999 with a bang by co-headlining the two-week Aussie Big Day Out festival with Hole and Marilyn Manson in the second half of January.

What with it being summer in Australia and *Follow the Leader*'s number-one debut on the continent nation's pop charts, Korn gladly agreed to join their old friends from Marilyn Manson on Australia's version of Lollapalooza. With acts such as the Fun Lovin' Criminals and Fatboy Slim slated to perform as well, the tour might have proved the exception to the rule that had seen Korn ostracized at one festival cafeteria after another.

Sadly, the only thing proved at the Big Day Out festival was that if Korn wanted to enjoy themselves while in transit, they had better pick the bands themselves. Not only did Courtney Love turn out to be a less-than-amiable consort, but Marilyn Manson effected a complete about-face, going so far as to actually bash Korn during his performance and baiting Jonathan to—among other things—suck his member. Courtney Love went in for more of the same, saying "I really like picking on Korn. I sort of turned it into an art form, and it made me really happy to pick on them, but then I realized that Jonathan is just kind of this loser, weak, sweet little guy." In fact, it seemed almost as if the two bands had bonded over their mutual distaste for Korn.

Taking none-too-kindly to his co-headliners' daily gibes, Jonathan chalked up the hostility to professional jealousy. According to the frontman, Manson's goading even led to blows at one point during the tour. "I thought it was funny," he later said, "because both those bands are so bitter and jealous towards us that all they did was talk about us and I just keep hearing all this talk. It was just getting ridiculous. Courtney said she made an art out of picking on us, and Manson said a whole bunch of stuff. I actually knocked him out onstage. He called me out, he said some pretty bad things about me in front of fifty thousand people, and I took him out right there onstage."

The singer had a point. Many was the night that Hole's show went down in flames. In fact, on several occasions Love actually had to lose her shirt to get a rise out of the Korn- and Manson-enamored audiences. Love's cognizance of her own strictly limited appeal was evidenced by the question she kept putting to the audience: "I can bring Korn back, you know—do you want Korn?"

That would be a definitive yes, judging by the crowd's reaction to Korn's appearance earlier in the day. From the Gold Coast to Sydney, to Melbourne to Perth, Australia got the quintessential Korn treatment. As soon as the guys wheeled their bikes onto the stage, the mosh pit would swell to catastrophic proportions. Everywhere the band went, broken arms and legs were guaranteed to follow. Despite the forty acts that played each day and the fusillade of cans, bottles, and shoes with which the fans showed their affection, Korn owned the stage and controlled the crowd, working the more than forty thousand spectators into an hourlong frenzy at every stop.

At the end of the Big Day Out, the backbiting of their tourmates couldn't overshadow Korn's supremacy. Their repertoire had featured songs from all three albums, and fans had taken to the new material as passionately as they had to the old. So what if Marilyn Manson was no longer playing the friend in Satan's clothing? Who cared if the infighting had spilled out onto the stage? In the States and abroad, Korn was still the mosher's gold standard.

11
krowned and dangerous

A hero's welcome greeted the Bakersfield Five upon their return to the States in early February. While *Follow the Leader* had turned platinum as early as September, the CD showed no signs of slowing down. Buoyed by the Family Values tour and the incessant airplay, the album would turn double-platinum within four weeks of the band's U.S. arrival. It must be noted that MTV also had a hand in augmenting the sales figures. Now that the station was no longer hell-bent on ignoring the guys' strident sound, they dedicated themselves to lauding the harbingers of the new evolution at every turn.

On Friday, February 5, 1999, the group was actually invited to mug for the same *Total Request Live* that has long been the province of the Spice Girls and their ilk. Some six months earlier, before MTV began hyping the living daylights out of "Got the Life," many Korn fans would have bet their Family Values tickets that the five rebels would have balked at such mass exposure. Of course, the fact is that Korn was no different than 99.9 percent of all underground phenomena, each breaking their backs to sell out, with varying degrees of success. As inevitably happens, once the media bigwigs began to warm up toward the concept of a band like Korn, lavishing them with copious amounts of print space and airtime, some of the group's earliest supporters began searching for the Next Big Thing.

Given the monumental effort that had gone into recording *Follow the Leader*, as well as their constant attempts to stay in touch with their followers, Korn could not in good conscience blame themselves for the loss of certain stalwarts. After all, trying to appease fans who make it their business—not to mention a point of fierce pride—to champion only those outfits that are on the fringe of the music industry would be an exercise in futility, and penury for a group of musicians at the peak of their powers.

And yet, the group had grown so fond of their place at the head of the countercultural table that they were loath to let it slip from their fingers. Displaying his reluctance to identify with all things pop-culture, Jonathan maintained, "The mainstream didn't want anything to do with us until this record. Even now, they give us the least amount of attention possible. They have to play us and write about us because it's gotten to the point of where it hurts them to ignore us. See, nobody on the inside really likes Korn. I think we'll always be on the outside, and from that point we're always looking in."

But the facts could not be denied. With the release of *Follow the Leader*, the band had not only gained a million new supporters, but also retained many more of their initial fans than they'd lost. All in all, not bad for a year's work. "The cool thing about Korn is that they take more fans in at the top but don't lose any at the bottom," explained Al Marasco, vice president of marketing at Epic Records. "That's the design of the band—they're built for the road. They're street-tough."

Thus it was with light hearts and a bounce in their step that the leaders of the doom-and-gloom generation sauntered into MTV headquarters in New York City to unveil the music video for their latest single, "Freak on a Leash." While the guys had shot the video over the course of two mid-December afternoons, it had taken weeks of painstaking effort to bring the directors' vision to fruition. No less than four directors had been retained to work on the chef d'oeuvre that would one day be hailed as the greatest rock video of the year, if not the decade. *Follow the Leader* cover artist Todd McFarlane had been charged with the task of expanding the illustration he'd sketched for the album into an animated short, while the directing team of Jonathan Dayton and Valerie Faris, who'd garnered numerous accolades through their work with Smashing Pumpkins, were brought on to develop the live-action sequence of the video along with Graham Morris.

Those with a taste for Korn were immediately struck by the video's agile merging of two distinct realities. The story, and the recondite moral thereof, provided food for thought for the band's fans and detractors alike. Picking up at the very scene that portrays a flaxen-haired girl playing hopscotch at the precipice of a cliff on the *Follow the Leader* cover, the video begins when a policeman accidentally fires a gun at the oblivious lassie. Just as the bullet is about to strike the child, it rips through the curtain of animation and enters real time where it proceeds to shatter glasses, lava lamps, and water coolers, pierces walls, tears through comic books, and punctures birthday-party balloons. At the end, the bullet returns to the animated scene of the crime, whereupon it stops before reaching its intended victim and lands in the palm of her hand. The young girl then hands the bullet back to the shamefaced policeman who'd fired it. Interspersed throughout are clips of Korn's high-voltage performance footage.

Not two weeks after its buzzworthy debut, "Freak on a Leash" had become an institution on the *Total Request*

Live countdown. An anomaly among representatives of the sunny Orlando sound, Korn finally had people asking, "Does this mean that the end of boy bands is at hand?" While Korn—who'd never missed an opportunity to slam all clean-cut popsters—would have liked nothing better than to respond in the affirmative, their management company, The Firm, had other ideas. Boosted by their success with Korn and Limp Bizkit, the company had just signed the diamond-selling Backstreet Boys—the coup of a lifetime, as it were.

The Firm's adroit management of Korn's stellar career track was again evidenced in the winter of 1999. After the Rob Zombie fiasco of the previous summer, many fans weighed in with their profound disappointment. It seemed that both Korn and Zombie aficionados had wanted nothing better than to see the two monsters of rock perform back-to-back. While Family Values had fared just fine without Rob Zombie, grossing nearly $240,000 per show, The Firm's gang of bloodhounds were quick to sniff out the trail of another sold-out tour. Taking the initiative, the management company struck a peace treaty with the Zombie camp, and a two-month tour, scheduled to begin in the last days of February, was promptly in the works.

To allay the public's confusion, the members of Korn took it upon themselves to explain their sudden change of attitude toward Rob Zombie. "There was a lot of misunderstandings involved," admitted David. "There was never any bad blood between us and Rob. Last summer it seemed as if there was some reluctance on his part to perform with certain artists—basically because he's a rock 'n' roll purist. But we got all that straightened out."

But what of Rob Zombie's insistence that it had only been his stage set, and not the choice of acts, that had determined his abrupt departure? Head conceded the point, saying, "He's so cool. We didn't have problems before, I think he just wanted to bring his stage set, and with all the bands on Family Values, I don't think it was really possible. It would have been hard for him to use everything. . . . Back then, when we were supposedly fighting with him about something, it was never us. We never even talked to him."

Presumably, now that the groups were talking, everyone was seeing eye-to-eye. Indeed, Zombie not only had consented to let his co-headliners play last, but he also agreed to plug Videodrone's new album by bringing the Elementree-signed artists on the road as a warm-up act. According to Head, the bands had come up with a system that would effectively eradicate any and all set-related problems. "Now we have Videodrone out with us, but they set up in front of Zombie. So Zombie set up in front and then we set up in back, and we turn the stage like we did on Family Values. He has the whole day for them to put up everything, then they just turn it around. So there's plenty of time so he can have his whole big, huge, haunted-house set. Everything he does he can fit onstage now, and timewise, everything works."

While stockpiling their energy reserves for the upcoming tour, Korn revealed that their relationship with Rob Zombie wasn't all that had changed with the passage of time. The group's stance on the live-album issue had also undergone a radical reconstruction since the summer of '98, when Fieldy and Jonathan claimed that they hated "live records. They sound like shit." Fieldy had also gone on to state that "there are bootleg live CDs. They suck, we don't get paid. [Bootleggers] are making more money than us!"

Prompted by the proliferation of substandard product, the band's shift in position was displayed by—what else?—a live CD. The *Family Values* album and accompanying home video would feature highlights from all six bands on the bill. Slated for release on March 30, 1999, the album would sell 121,000 in its first week on the market, debut at number 7 on the *Billboard* 200 and console Korn, as well as all interested parties, for the loss of countless dollars through bootleg live albums.

Although the band would remain the most industrious act in music, their tour itineraries would also need to undergo an overhaul now that they no longer had to rely strictly on word of mouth for the selling of their albums and the housing and feeding of their ever-expanding families. Prior to the release of *Follow the Leader*, the guys had planned to tour for at least eighteen months, albeit not as intensely as in seasons past. "We'll probably tour for a year and a half, two years," Fieldy had said. "At least," Jonathan continued. "We'll be doing our same touring but at least we'll have the ability to fly, keep our heads straight. Have a day off every three days."

The runaway success of Korn's third album, the minute-by-minute media coverage, the heavy rotation and the sold-out Family Values tour package put the kibosh on all such plans. *Follow the Leader* would keep flying off the shelves, regardless of whether Korn toured to support it or not. In light of these recent developments, the quintet made the unanimous decision to stop the buses after the tour with Zombie, and return to the studio for album number four. Even more surprisingly, the group chose not to put out a third single. This, despite the public's rampant speculation and anticipation. "Actually, we're going in to write a new record June first," Brian relayed. "We're gonna disappear for a little bit and give people a break. We don't want to beat the record to death, put out a third single, a fourth single, and have people going, 'Enough already!' "

With their fourth album, Korn intended to take full advantage of their new position of power. In the eyes of fans who'd arrived on the heels of *Follow the Leader*, Korn knew they could do no wrong. This latest opus would be for all those masses disgruntled by the band's departures from the raw strength and heavy groove of pre-yesteryear. Standing at the helm of the new hardcore movement, the band planned to pick up where *Korn* left off.

On February 26, 1999, with their minds already fixated on the studio, Korn boarded their Middle America–bound tour bus for the inception of their trek alongside Rob Zombie. The groups dubbed their tour "Rock Is Dead," thereby piquing the ire of Marilyn Manson, who had a song of the same name on his *Mechanical Animals* CD. (Later, a fuming Manson decided to dispense with the unspoken "first tour, first title" courtesy, naming his spring tour "Rock Is Dead" as well.) Traveling with the pyromaniacal Rob Zombie, whose set featured topless dancers, Charles Manson imagery, and enough explosions to make the workings of Mrs. O'Leary's cow look like a grease fire, Korn reckoned they'd need more than Jonathan's kilt-and-bagpipe combination to bring down the house. While nothing could rival Zombie's massive showcase, the Korn cage concept was certainly a clever enough beginning,

Before every show, Korn's stagehands would set up a giant cage as their backdrop. Then the roadies would be sent to scare up a Krowd of Korn kids who cared enough to spend an hour examining the kernels' backsides from behind bars. Those who consented—and there was never a shortage of takers—were ushered into captivity immediately after the Zombie show. Not to be outdone by Dragula's antics, Korn also enlisted their own caravan of strippers to corrupt the minds of young audiences.

Except for the tour's second stop in Albuquerque, New Mexico, where a broken equipment rider ensured that the show would have to go on late and without the benefit of stage gear, the Rock Is Dead juggernaut proceeded from one arena to the next without hitting a snag. That is, unless one considers poison-pen concert reviews any kind of impediment. But while many of the overworked and underpaid critics picked this as their time to lambaste the band for a "mundane," "bland," and "low-energy" performance, the capacity crowds never seemed to notice, moshing, pogoing, and body-surfing with the bacchanalian glee characteristic of true concertgoers. After witnessing such an outpouring of affection, Korn had no need to scour the local papers for positive affirmation, much less for dissenting opinions.

For Korn, as well as for their fellow Bako boys in Videodrone, the most important date of the tour had to be April 14, 1999. Ty Elam, Videodrone's frontman, confirmed that it was in fact "the most anticipated part of the tour, for us and for Korn." Playing in Bakersfield's huge Centennial Garden arena, the groups bore witness to a sold-out venue rocking with the bodies of friends and foes alike. No longer the outcast of yore, Jonathan would have liked to think that some of those cheerleaders and jocks who'd mocked him back in the day were in the audience, cursing their fates and pumping their fists to the sounds of "A.D.I.D.A.S." and "Faget."

The bands took a day to unwind and hang with the homies after the Bakersfield performance, resuming their trek in Anaheim on April 16. With only ten days left to go, the tour was already being hailed as a commercial triumph. But on every parade a little rain must fall. While the ticket-sales figures would indeed come back overwhelmingly positive, the tour would not end on the high note presaged by such a windfall. On Friday, April 23, the band was playing to another jacked-up crowd at the Kempner Arena when David began to feel a numbness creeping over his hand and arm. While the beat-keeper's fierce performances had always left him physically drained, this was different. By the end of the show, David felt as if he couldn't so much as grip his stick, much less drum through a whole song.

As the audience roared for an encore, expecting the band to reemerge and close the show with their rendition of "Earache My Eye" as they had done at every other Rock Is Dead stop, the guys were backstage, scrambling to figure out what manner of affliction had beset David's aching arm. Conferring with doctors, they learned that the stickman would have to stay off the skins and snares if he wanted to get his hands back in working order in time to record Korn's follow-up to *Follow the Leader*. "David was experiencing some numbness in one of his hands, and was having trouble gripping his stick [thus making playing rather difficult]," a representative from The Firm later confirmed. "He's fine, has seen a doctor, and there are no permanent problems."

Still, there was no possibility of giving the fervent Kansas crowd an encore. Neither would the tour continue as scheduled. To the great disappointment of Korn fans all over the Midwest, the two final shows in St. Louis and Indianapolis also had to be canceled.

With David nursing his fatigued wrist through most of May, the guys were able to relax with the baby Korns, hit the strip clubs, think about their imminent studio venture, and reflect upon the events of the past twelve months. Considering all that had come to pass, there was no shortage of food for thought. After all, it hadn't been a year since they'd first broken through to mainstream audiences. In the months that had followed, they had launched their own annual package tour. Orgy's *Candy-ass*, the first album to be released by their record label, had at last turned gold. The biggest names in hip-hop, such as Ice Cube, Outkast, Naughty by Nature, and Wu-Tang Clan, had embraced their genre-splicing efforts. They'd inked a deal, reportedly in the high six figures, with Adidas archnemeses at Puma, Inc., and changed their style accordingly. They'd guested on several of their friends' albums, not the least of which was Limp Bizkit's triple-platinum-within-two-months-of-release *Significant Other*, and appeared on a host of compilation CDs. To cap it all off, there was the invitation to take their rightful place among the recording industry's best and brightest at Woodstock '99. All in all, a smashing year for a band that had been overlooked by the Grammys. Indeed the general consensus seemed to be that Korn had single-handedly rescued hard guitar rock from the clutches of irrelevance.

A year such as this can elicit but a single question: "Now what?" Pondering the direction of their fourth album, the group soon hit upon the concept that would serve to define fin-de-siècle Korn. In the grand tradition of the Who's *Tommy* and the Fugees' *The Score*, the tracks on Korn's fourth installment would combine into one cohesive tale of Jonathan's struggles with drugs and alcohol. As such, the LP would not include any guest stars. "There's no guests on this album because Jonathan is writing this album as one story, from the beginning to the end," explained Fieldy, "so it wouldn't make sense if someone came in and guest-appeared in the middle of the record. It would be like, he's telling a story, then all of a sudden there's a rap guest or something weird in there. It just wouldn't make sense. Not that we wouldn't like to, it just doesn't make sense for this record . . . And if we do, then it's going to be a hidden track. So there's not anybody in mind right now."

On board to produce the record was sometime Pearl Jam, Rage Against the Machine and Stone Temple Pilots producer Brendan O'Brian, who'd also mixed *Follow the Leader*. With their Los Angeles rehearsal studio booked through August, the group spent May raring to pour their creative juices into the heaviest tracks ever to defile the naked ear. All the pieces were in place when the band began pre-production on June 3, 1999. Unlike the drawn-out production process that had stalled the release of the last album, recording this latest effort would be a brisk business. As if aiming for the title of Most Prolific Outfit in Rock, band, label, and management alike had their sights set on a late-1999 release date.

Going strictly by the band's descriptions, fans could expect an album that would take them for the anti-joyride of the century. "It's really heavy this time . . . It's like if we were to record the first Korn album today," Fieldy promised. Concurring with his bass player, Jonathan added, " 'Cause back in the day, that was the heaviest. When *Korn* came out, that was our newest, heaviest stuff. It was dark, it was going on."

Sure enough, the forces of inspiration colluded with the musicians, helping them to write eight songs in the first two weeks of pre-production. Since the band's belief in the power of the Internet had not waned any since the days of the *Korn After-School Special*, Jonathan still made a point of providing fans with weekly updates through the www.Korn.com Web site. Through these postings, many fans learned that most of the tracks had been worked out as early as July 20. Save for one unavoidable engagement, the band was ready to enter the recording studio.

While Woodstock '99 would turn out to be less a celebration of the original event than a miserable failure of an attempt to capitalize upon the success of Woodstock

'94, Korn could not pass up the opportunity to play before a crowd 250,000 strong. The list of participating acts read like a who's who of modern rock, and with everybody who was anybody scheduled to perform, Korn quickly made Woodstock the exception to the outdoor shows they'd all but sworn off since conceiving of Family Values. After all, with 1 percent of America's entire teen population slated to attend the three-day festival, and countless more expected to tune in for the round-the-clock coverage on pay-per-view, the eyes of the world would rest squarely on Korn for the duration of their hourlong set. All combined, Woodstock was an offer few bands could refuse.

To prepare for the biggest show of their career, Korn mounted two considerably smaller, warm-up shows at L.A.'s Whisky-a-Go-Go on July 20 and 21. Then, on Friday, July 23, the first day of Woodstock, the group flew to upstate New York where they were due to play at nine o'clock that evening. Like most bands on the roster, they planned to arrive at the defunct Griffis Air Force Base–cum–concert venue just in time to take their places, do all they could to instigate widespread chaos, and go home before the next band hit the stage—especially since that band was none other than Bush, the dreaded representatives of Brit-grunge.

Leading up to Korn's set were acts such as Jamiroquai, Sheryl Crow, Līve, DMX, and the Offspring. For all the insults that Korn have hurled at their punk asses, the latter band did a great deal to prep the aggressive crowd for their kindred-spirit rockers. But while the Offspring got the mosh pit moving, Korn were the ones who set it into limb-breaking, head-gashing motion. Pulling two new songs off their forthcoming LP, the group ensured that no album went underrepresented, with renditions of "Blind," "A.D.I.D.A.S." and "Got the Life." For an hour, they rocked the East Stage with a ferocity that resonated through every orifice of the Rome, New York, former air force base, and invaded the home of every Woodstock pay-TV subscriber. According to one of the event's medical volunteers, "When Korn came on, people were coming in every three minutes on stretchers." Jonathan, on the other hand, reckoned that "it was the best Korn show we've ever done."

Never before had the band seen a pit of such monstrous proportions. For the men onstage, the wave of unconditional adulation provided a rush of unprecedented magnitude. But for the people who watched, reported on, and heard of the carnage, the festival was either an abomination of the Almighty, or proof positive of civilization's path toward self-destruction. Within two days of Korn's show, Woodstock '99 would erupt into riots and conflagrations. The unsanitary conditions, the high price of drinking water, the understaffed security team, and the inescapable heat would turn music lover against music lover, and send baby-boomers into a rousing chorus of "What's the Matter with Kids Today?" *Spin* and *Rolling Stone* would write stories on the bloodbath, recording the innumerable gang rapes, drug overdoses, frenzied riots, and general mob-rule in harrowing detail. Fingers would be pointed at Korn as well as at Limp Bizkit, but the buck would have to stop at the offices of the unfeeling concert promoters, who'd multiplied $150 by 250,000, and then added in revenues from pay-per-view and concessions to arrive at a take-home figure that would more than offset the price of talent, staff, and a few scarred-for-life guests.

Much as the U.S. media would have liked to lump Korn in with the rest of Woodstock's atrocities, the fact is that the band has always defied such simple-minded categorization. In striking contrast to the scene in Rome, New York, the guys' homes in Huntington Beach and Long

Beach were the site of frolicking children and expecting homemakers. Indeed, upon Korn's return to L.A., David found his wife Shannon two contractions away from childbirth. On July 27, she gave birth to Sophia Aurora Silveria, a playmate for two-year-old David Silveria Jr., and the apple of her father's eye.

After his daughter's arrival, David and the band entered the recording studio to begin cutting tracks for their fourth and still-untitled studio album. Still shaking their heads and refusing to comment on the apocalyptic outcome of Woodstock, the musicians got a call from their management, informing them of an unlikely source of support. Apparently, the folks at MTV were now Korn's number one fans, bestowing "Freak on a Leash" with a staggering nine nominations for the MTV Video Music Awards. Korn were the most-nominated artists of the year.

By now, the days of MTV shunning our five heroes had become a thing of the all-but-forgotten past. Except for cutting out the curse words and bowing to outraged parental groups by showing only snippets of the "Freak on a Leash" video after the May 18 massacre at Columbine High School in Littleton, Colorado, MTV had adopted the lords of New Metal with open arms. Videos from Korn, as well as Kid Rock and Limp Bizkit, were now staples of the MTV diet. The Bakersfield Five had created the movement that defined the turn-of-the-century zeitgeist, and with the 1999 MTV Video Music Awards ceremony being hyped as the last of the millennium, it seemed only fitting to recognize the pace-setting quintet's massive contribution.

Not two weeks before the MTV nominations were unveiled, Korn had asserted their predominance in an altogether different, and substantially newer, medium. On July 16, 1999, the guys took home the first-ever CDDB

Silicon CD Award. CDDB (an acronym for CD Database) had tracked Korn's *Follow the Leader* as the most widely played CD on the Internet. With all these honors and the Korn flag flying high over the heads of Generation Next, could the elusive Grammy be far behind? Suffice it to say, the guys are still hoping.

With the recording of their fourth studio venture running a smooth course in Los Angeles and Atlanta, Georgia, the press was at last notified of a firm, November 17 release date. Working toward their deadline, the group would have little time for either concerts or press, not to mention family. Of course, they'd make an adjustment for the MTV Video Music Awards on—drumroll please—9/9/99. On an overcast New York afternoon, the Metropolitan Opera House in Manhattan's Lincoln Center was the self-proclaimed center of the world. To wit, New York City streets had been renamed after various rock, rap, and pop stars in honor of the occasion.

As always, the forces of nature refused to cooperate with the power hitters–that–be. Rain spilled down with the same disregard for the well-groomed coifs of the nominees as for the unwashed tresses of the clamoring masses. Eventually the showers let up, and Jonathan, a vision in white polyester-blend tracksuit and top hat, could give interviews with his casually-attired bandmates without fear of looking like the winner of a wet T-shirt contest. While most of the banter revolved around the conspicuously Kornless second annual Family Values trek, the guys' minds were on the awards show.

In a pre-show announcement, it was revealed that "Freak on a Leash" had already won for Best Editing in a Video, while losing out on the accolades for Best Cinematography, Special Effects, and Art Direction. But that tally still left Korn with five nominations—namely, for

Video of the Year, Best Rock Video, Viewers' Choice, Best Direction in a Video, and Breakthrough Video. With plenty of empty space on their mantels, the guys wanted those MTV moonmen, if only as surrogate Grammys. Most of all, they wanted their moment at the mike. If they won, it would be their first time accepting an award on a nationally televised program.

Once inside, the musicians were seated in a prime row, right behind Will Smith, Eminem, and Dr. Dre. With a bevy of beautiful wives at their sides, the guys watched as their nominations translated into awards for other artists. However, when Tommy Lee and Christina Aguilera emerged to present the award for Best Rock Video, everyone knew that at least one of the evening's many losing streaks was about to come to an abrupt end. Not that the competition wasn't steep. Going up against Lenny Kravitz's instant classic, "Fly Away," Limp Bizkit's and Kid Rock's star-making "Nookie" and "Bamwitdaba" respectively, as well as the high-camp factor of the Offspring's "Pretty Fly (for a White Guy)," the Best Rock Video award could easily have been another in a series of disappointments. Keeping their expectations in check, David, Head, Fieldy, Jonathan, and Munky white-knuckled their way through the introduction.

"And the winner is"—began Aguilera—"Korn, 'Freak on a Leash'!"

And they were up. Jonathan's ivory form was the first to come ripping out of its seat, both fists in the air. In all the excitement, he was in the aisle before Renée could even flash him the look that clearly said, "Look, David is kissing *his* wife." Sure enough, the platinum-haired drummer was holding up the others, locking lips with a statuesque redhead. At length, all five Bako boys were on the stage, hugging each other, expressing the depth of their emotion, and leaving no doubt as to whether they had actually thought it an honor just to be nominated.

Munky was the first to cut through the public display of affection.

"I'd like to thank this band right here for being the hardest-working band in rock 'n' roll," he told the audience.

Snapping back into his role as Korn's unofficial spokesperson, Jonathan stepped up to the podium and thanked the video directors but for whom none of this would have been possible.

"We also want to thank all our fans out there," he continued, " 'cause it's been a long, long hard road for us. We started way back, years ago—people don't really know that—and it's been a long, hard road, and I can't believe we finally got this, and we just want to thank you so much."

The task of thanking families, crew, and colleagues fell to David's considerably calmer countenance.

"Everyone we've worked with has fought for us since day one," he said. "We got the best record label in the industry, Immortal/Epic . . . Our management, the same thing, the best in the business . . . But most of all—Korn kids. The best. The best support ever. We love you guys."

What more need be said of Korn and the secret of their success? The next day, the group would be back in an Atlanta, Georgia, recording studio, working on their highly anticipated album. Let us not pretend that the binding of these pages can encapsulate what is sure to be a long and eventful career. Even as you read this, Korn are in the process of planning another album. Whether fans and fortune will smile upon their future efforts as they have on albums past, is for you the people to decide and for biographers other than this one to document. The fact

of Korn's indelible impact upon the music scene remains
the sole certainty. Like an asteroid, they came out of nowhere, traversing tremendous distances at the speed of
light to show up as a blip on the periphery of the cultural
radar. Even then, no one save a few so-called madmen believed that a day would come when Korn would leave a
dent the size of the Grand Canyon on the very face of the
rock 'n' roll landscape, wipe out any signs of the Mesozoic
era (read, Grunge Age), and give rise to a brand-new spe-
cies of rock band. In these eyes, if not always in their own,
they've earned the right to wear the laurel wreath for life.
To quote Jonathan, "There's tons [of imitators] . . . But
we'll always have that we fuckin' created it."

acknowledgments

First and foremost, this book could not have been written without the numerous journalists and publications who had the good taste and foresight to follow the band since its inception. My thanks goes out to the earliest Korn supporters at *Mörat Kerrang!*, *Circus*, and *Metal Hammer*. The following sources also provided a wealth of information: *East Coast Rocker*, *Guitar Player* magazine, *Guitar World*, *Modern Drummer*, *Metal Maniacs*, *Pit* magazine, *Hit Parader*, Associated Press, Minneapolis *Star Tribune*, *Los Angeles Times*, *Spin*, *Rolling Stone*, *Metal Edge*, *The Buzz*, *Datebook*, *Dotmusic*, *Epic Media* magazine, *Ticketmaster*, *Entertainment Weekly*, *Guitar* magazine, *Allstar*, *Business Wire*, *Addicted to Noise*—the on-line rock 'n' roll magazine—and finally, the comprehensive archives of the MTV news gallery.

My most effusive thanks must go to my editor, Joe Veltre, as well as Erika Fad, and my agent, Giles Anderson. As always, Mira and Elina helped in ways I couldn't even begin to recount. Finally, John Nikkah, for his tireless research efforts, and Roman, for being the only person I know who still thinks Korn is a vegetable.

Furman, Leah.

Korn.

30656002019944

$11.95

6/2000		DATE	

about the author

Leah Furman is the author of numerous biographies.
She lives and writes in New York City.